Eva-Marie Großkurth, Jürgen Handke (Eds.)

The Inverted Classroom Model

Also of Interest

Informatik und Gesellschaft
Andrea Kienle, Gabriele Kunau, 2014
ISBN 978-3-486-73597-0, e-ISBN 978-3-486-78145-8,
e-ISBN (ePUB) 978-3-486-99058-4

Mensch-Maschine-Interaktion
Andreas Butz, Antonio Krüger, 2014
ISBN 978-3-486-71621-4, e-ISBN 978-3-486-71967-3,
e-ISBN (ePUB) 978-3-486-98971-7

Prozessführungssysteme
Michael Herczeg, 2014
ISBN 978-3-486-58445-5, e-ISBN 978-3-486-72005-1,
e-ISBN (ePUB) 978-3-486-98969-4, Set-ISBN 978-3-486-79087-0

Mensch und Computer 2014 – Tagungsband
Michael Koch, Andreas Butz, Johann Schlichter (Eds.), 2014
ISBN 978-3-11-034415-8, e-ISBN 978-3-11-034448-6,
e-ISBN (ePUB) 978-3-11-039661-4, Set-ISBN 978-3-11-034449-3

Mediendidaktik, 4. Auflage
Michael Kerres, 2013
ISBN 978-3-486-73602-1, e-ISBN 978-3-486-73603-8

The Inverted Classroom Model

The 3rd German ICM-Conference – Proceedings

Edited by Eva-Marie Großkurth, Jürgen Handke

DE GRUYTER
OLDENBOURG

Editors

Eva-Marie Großkurth
Philipps-Universität Marburg
Institut für Anglistik und Amerikanistik
Wilhelm-Röpke-Str. 6D
35032 Marburg
eva.grosskurth@staff.uni-marburg.de

Prof. Dr. Jürgen Handke
Philipps-Universität Marburg
Institut für Anglistik und Amerikanistik
Wilhelm-Röpke-Str. 6D
35032 Marburg
handke@staff.uni-marburg.de

ISBN 978-3-11-034417-2
e-ISBN (PDF) 978-3-11-034446-2
e-ISBN (EPUB) 978-3-11-039660-7
Set-ISBN 978-3-11-034447-9

Bibliographic information published by the Deutsche Nationalbibliothek
The Deutsche Nationalbibliothek lists this publication in the Deutsche Nationalbibliografie; detailed bibliographic data are available on the Internet at http://dnb.dnb.de.

Cover illustration: Wavebreakmedia Ltd/Wavebreak Media/Thinkstock
Printing and binding: CPI books GmbH, Leck
♾ Printed on acid-free paper
Printed in Germany

www.degruyter.com

Contents

Preface

Only two years after its first run, the *Inverted Classroom* Conference had become a familiar event at Marburg University. Most conference participants in February 2014 not only knew about this digital teaching and learning scenario but had been experienced users and developers. They had hands-on experience, they could report on new variants of in-class scenarios, they had conducted small- and large-scale *Inverted Classroom* projects, and some of them now even could present their evaluation results – in short, most of the conference participants were now not only familiar with the model but had developed variants in order to adapt the model to their subjects and their needs.

Whereas in its predecessors, most participants wanted to familiarize themselves with the central components of the *Inverted Classroom Model*, the focus of the 3rd German *Inverted Classroom* Conference to which this conference volume is dedicated was not only a discussion of several variants of the model but also, for the first time, the inclusion of long-term evaluations and aspects of student behavior.

This shift of emphasis is refelected in the contributions to this volume. Even though still all central aspects of the ICM are addressed, content production and delivery, testing, and the in-class phase, we can now find recommendations concerning acquisition of digital material, in-class tuition, the role of student tutors as well as first long-term studies about ICM-effects.

In general then, the focus was much wider than that of the first two ICM-conferences: From a new and originally non-familiar teaching and learning scenario to more general aspects of digitization of teaching and learning in the 21st century.

And what about 2015? Honestly, we do not know. No one could predict the direction that eventually was taken in the 2014 conference. We were all caught by surprise by the different approaches taken and we were delighted to learn how innovatively teachers from across the country had been using the basic model. Thus, for 2015 we cannot make any predictions. However one aspect can now be taken for granted: The ICM has now become an established and suitable model for coping with the challenges of 21st century teaching and learning.

Eva-Marie Großkurth, Jürgen Handke

Marburg, August 2014

The Authors

Eva-Marie Großkurth
Philipps-Universität Marburg
Institut für Anglistik und Amerikanistik
Wilhelm-Röpke-Str. 6D
35032 Marburg
E-Mail: eva.grosskurth@staff.uni-marburg.de

Prof. Dr. Jürgen Handke
Philipps-Universität Marburg
Institut für Anglistik und Amerikanistik
Wilhelm-Röpke-Str. 6D
35032 Marburg
E-Mail: handke@staff.uni-marburg.de
Lectures online: http://www.youtube.com/linguisticsmarburg
Website: http://www.linguistics-online.com

Stephan Beier, M.A.
Hamburg University of Applied Sciences
Faculty of Business & Social Affairs
Department of Business
Berliner Tor 5
20099 Hamburg
E-Mail: stephan.beier@haw-hamburg.de

Himanshi Braun
E-Learning-Service
Georg-August-Universität Göttingen
Platz der Göttinger Sieben 5
37073 Göttingen

Vicdan Burna
Hochschule Heilbronn
c/o Kerstin Raudonat
Max-Planck-Str. 39
74081 Heilbronn
E-Mail: vburna@stud.hs-heilbronn.de

Prof. Dr. Christian Decker
Hamburg University of Applied Sciences
Faculty of Business & Social Affairs
Department of Business
Berliner Tor 5
20099 Hamburg
E-Mail: christian.decker@haw-hamburg.de

Jennifer Floyd, M.A.
E-Mail: jlouflo@gmail.com

Dominikus Herzberg
Technische Hochschule Mittelhessen
Wiesenstraße 14
35390 Gießen
E-Mail: dominikus.herzberg@mni.thm.de
Website:http://www.mni.thm.de/index.php/component/thm_groups/profile/default/2877-Herzberg

Oliver Kreutz
Juristische Fakultät
Georg-August-Universität Göttingen
Platz der Göttinger Sieben 6
37073 Göttingen

Prof. Dr. Volkmar Langer
Hochschule Weserbergland
Am Stockhof 2
31785 Hameln
E-Mail: langer@hsw-hameln.de
Website: www.hsw-hameln.de

Knut Linke
Hochschule Weserbergland
Am Stockhof 2
31785 Hameln
E-Mail: linke@hsw-hameln.de
Website: www.hsw-hameln.de

Nicola Marsden
Fakultät für Informatik
Hochschule Heilbronn
Max-Planck-Str. 39
74081 Heilbronn
Website: www.hs-heilbronn.de/nicola.marsden
E-Mail: nicola.marsden@hs-heilbronn.de

Philip Meyer
Projekt „e-teaching·org im Kontext sozialer Netzwerke“
Stiftung Medien in der Bildung (SbR)
IWM - Leibniz-Institut für Wissensmedien
Schleichstr. 6
72076 Tübingen
E-Mail: p.meyer@iwm-kmrc.de

Anja Penßler-Beyer
Auf der Weide 24
35037 Marburg
E-Mail: penssler@students.uni-marburg.de

Kerstin Raudonat
Fakultät für Informatik
Hochschule Heilbronn
Max-Planck-Str. 39
74081 Heilbronn
E-Mail: kerstin.raudonat@hs-heilbronn.de
Website: www.hs-heilbronn.de/kerstin.raudonat

Almut Reiners
E-Learning-Service
Georg-August-Universität Göttingen
Platz der Göttinger Sieben 5
37073 Göttingen

Dominik Rudisch
Hochschule Heilbronn
c/o Kerstin Raudonat
Max-Planck-Str. 39
E-Mail: drudisch@stud.hs-heilbronn.de

Florian Schimanke
Hochschule Weserbergland
Am Stockhof 2
31785 Hameln
E-Mail: schimanke@hsw-hameln.de
Website: www.hsw-hameln.de

Selma Ulusoy
Hochschule Heilbronn
c/o Kerstin Raudonat
Max-Planck-Str. 39
74081 Heilbronn
E-Mail: sulusoy@stud.hs-heilbronn.de

Prof. Dr. Andreas Wiebe
Juristische Fakultät
Georg-August-Universität Göttingen
Platz der Göttinger Sieben 6
37073 Göttingen

Katharina Weber
Geschwister-Scholl-Str. 3/306
35039 Marburg
E-Mail: kawe@gmail.com

Dirk Weidmann
Website: http://weidmanndirk.wordpress.com/
Blog: http://lernhelfer.wordpress.com/
E-Mail: weidmanndirk@googlemail.com

Mareike Wempen
Auf dem Wehr 27
35039 Marburg
E-Mail: wempen@students.uni-marburg.de

Fabian Wiedenhöfer
Hochschule Heilbronn
c/o Kerstin Raudonat
Max-Planck-Str. 39
74081 Heilbronn
E-Mail: fwiedenh@stud.hs-heilbronn.de

Sabrina Zeaiter, M.A.
Philipps-Universität Marburg
Institut für Anglistik und Amerikanistik
Wilhelm-Röpke-Str. 6D
35032 Marburg
E-Mail: sabrina.zeaiter@staff.uni-marburg.de

I Evaluation and Empirical Evidence of ICM Implementation

For the first time long-term evaluations and empirical research which have been conducted during the last semesters constitute contributions to these 3rd ICM conference proceedings.

Based on empirical research, Christian Decker and Stephan Beier answer the central question whether the implementation of the ICM, with its learner-centered self-navigation, its intensification of cooperation, and the learners' active involvement in the learning process, lead to an increased learning success compared to traditional teaching methods. Their evaluation of the ICM implementation at the HAW Hamburg shows that a higher learning success and an enhancement of learner-centered self-guidance and active participation and collaboration are the results.

Similar beneficiary effects are shown by Jürgen Handke in his evaluation of two on-campus classes and the VLC-MOOC 'Linguistics 201'. Supported by a wealth of data, he gives an overview on general student behavior, in-class attendance and learning outcomes in large classes with regard to special adjustments to the *Inverted Classroom Mastery Model.*

1 The Instructor as Navigator: Empirical Evidence of the Implementation of the ICM at HAW Hamburg

Christian Decker & Stephan Beier

1.1 Introduction

The Hamburg University of Applied Sciences (HAW Hamburg) is the third largest University of Applied Sciences in Germany. At HAW Hamburg, curricula of three different bachelor degree programmes include the identical lecture module 'Investment and Finance'. The three programmes are:

- Foreign Trade/International Management
- Logistics/Technical Business Administration, and
- Marketing/Technical Business Administration

In the summer semester 2013, the *Inverted Classroom Model* (ICM) was introduced. The implementation of the ICM was accompanied by an empirical research project. The research question to be investigated was whether the implementation of the ICM, with its learner-centered self-navigation, its intensification of cooperation, and the learners' active involvement in the learning process, lead to an increased learning success compared to traditional teaching methods. A master thesis, which was conducted in the context of the degree programme 'Educational Media' at the University Duisburg-Essen, documents the results of this research project.

1.2 Initial situation

The lecture module 'Investment and Finance', which combines the two sub-modules 'Investment' and 'Finance', is credited with 5 ECTS credit points (2.5 ECTS-CP each). The lectures of the sub-module 'Finance' comprise 15 weekly sessions (90 minutes each), taught separately for each of the three degree programmes. The average number of students enrolled in the three programmes totals to approximately 140 to 170 students per semester. Previously, the lecture contained both parts of traditional teacher-focused reading and parts of hands-on seminars. However, significant parts of the lecture were characterised by elements of traditional teaching approaches. Between 30 and 60 students participated regularly in each session. In general, the students did not have previous lecture-specific or practical knowledge. In the past, the average failure rate had continuously increased to reach a peak of 57%. Assumed drivers for this trend were the distinctive heterogeneity with respect to the individual cognitive capacity, the abilities of concentration and reflection, the motivation, and the social behaviour. However, the lecture module's evaluations in the past indicated that an increased portion of practical-based case studies and hands-on exercises might have positive effects on the students' motivation, which might also impact the students' learning success and examination grades. Due to time constraints, such an increase in activities would have resulted in a reduced content of reading, which might have induced problems with the accreditation of the study programmes.

1.3 Development of a new concept

Based upon the observation of the initial situation, it was analysed whether the course concept could be modified in order to improve the lecture's quality and accordingly better meet the students' needs. These aims ought to be achieved by shifting the focus of learning from teacher-centered lectures towards student-centered learning activities. Furthermore, the modification of the concept was supposed to be realised without the reduction of the content of learning. Didactical and methodical changes in the course concept were based on the *Inverted Classroom Model* (Schäfer, 2012: 3). The modified concept should define the framework for an increase in the students' intensified and self-directed learning engagement (Davis, 2013: 214) as well as an increase of their responsibility for learning processes (Spannagel, 2012: 73). Furthermore, the modified concept should increase the students' involvement in constructivist learning environments such as active and collaborative learning activities (Bishop/Verleger, 2013). In this concept, the provision of e-learning videos during the online phase should mainly support self-directed learning processes and their positive impacts on cognition and information processing as well as motivation and flexible handling of resources regarding time and place (Friedrich/Mandl, 1997). Activities during the in-class phases should mainly be based on constructivist learning environments such as active, cooperative and problem-based learning approaches (Bishop/Verleger, 2013). The graphic below presents the theoretical framework of the new course concept.

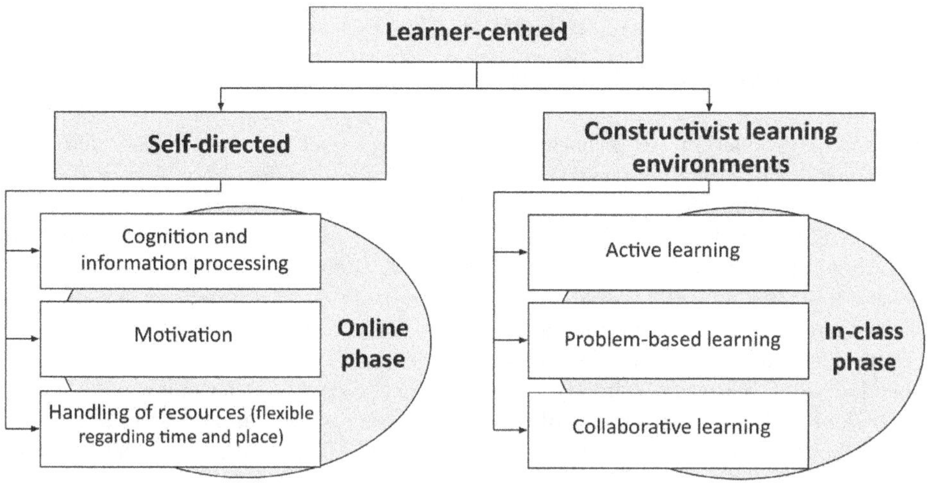

Figure 1.1: Framework for a learner-centered concept in the 'Finance'-lecture

The development of a fundamental theoretical understanding and the acquisition of practical and methodical competencies were major objectives while developing the course concept. It was expected that students comprehend the teaching and learning content at a deeper level and that failure rates decrease. Finally, the new concept was supposed to lead to an improvement of the students' learning success. Therefore, four hypotheses were derived from the research of learning theories with regard to the implementation of self-directed, active and collaborative learning activities, which ought to be realised by the application of the *Inverted Classroom Model*:

(1) The transfer of self-guiding and self-responsibility leads to a more intensive engagement with the learning content compared to traditional teaching approaches.

(2) The design of in-class phases leads to intensified active participation as well as to intensified collaboration and cooperative learning activities.

(3) Students intensifying their active involvement or achieving a better understanding of contents prefer the concept compared to traditional teaching approaches.

(4) The implementation of an ICM leads to increased learning success, which may range from a better understanding of the learning contents to better average examination results.

The analysis of the hypotheses was subject to empirical research based on the lecture module 'Finance' at HAW Hamburg in the summer semester 2013.

1.4 Content production and distribution and organisation of in-class activities

The content production for e-learning videos was based on an extensive *Microsoft PowerPoint* script containing various graphics, charts, drawings, pictures, explications and definitions. The script was exclusively developed for the implementation of the new course concept under consideration of underlying learning objectives. Graphical animations and narrative audio explications were added by using a rapid e-learning software tool. In total, illustrative video lectures of about 800 minutes were produced. For the purpose of the student's identification with the content, important segments such as chapter introductions and summaries were designed to feature the lecturer, who, in embedded video sequences, directly addresses the audience. Furthermore, the e-learning videos were enriched with additional didactical elements such as formative assessments (Handke/Schäfer, 2012: 151). At the end of each sub-chapter, the videos included computer generated quizzes and associated assessments in order to keep students active and focused on the learning (Loviscach, 2013: 8). The quizzes should serve as important elements to support the students' self-directed learning processes.

In addition to e-learning videos, students were also provided with a large set of associated assignments, exercises, questions for reflection and recapitulation, research tasks and case studies, which partly formed the subject of in-class activities during the course. Providing a detailed study guide finally linked e-learning videos and additional course materials. The study guide described the complete course concept and the learning objectives. Furthermore, it provided a detailed outline and approximate time schedule for in-class activities and topics to facilitate the students' focused preparation for in-class activities. The entire set of learning materials was provided via an internet-based learning management system. In order to increase the students' ability of self-direction, all materials were made accessible from the first day at the beginning of the semester rather than provided sequentially throughout the course. In addition to the distribution function for learning materials, the learning management systems administrated a communication function for asynchronous communication between course participants. The installation of different kinds of forums enabled internet-based discussions. However, the students' limited use of this feature indicated further potential for improvement.

The regular in-class participation was voluntary for students. However, it was expected that students were prepared for the respective topics. Conceptually, in-class time was based on student-focused discussions, problem-based group works, collaborative activities, and methods such as the *Think-Pair-Share*-Approach (Lyman, 1981) or the *Active Auditorium* or *Active Plenum* (Spannagel, 2011). In-class activities primarily dealt with content based on materials distributed in advance. Besides, students were partly provided with additional unknown exercises. The task of the lecturer was not the presentation of content, but the best possible support of students during their individual learning progress.

1.5 Collection of empirical information

Empirical information for the discussion of the research question was collected and analysed during the initial implementation of the course in summer semester 2013. Empirical information mainly stems from four resources:

(1) The department of quality control at HAW Hamburg regularly conducts the evaluation of lectures. This evaluation is based on a standard questionnaire containing multiple choice questions and open questions. However, the standard questionnaire made it difficult to collect appropriate information for an analysis of the research question. Only two open questions served the aim of the research project. The questions enabled students to provide a feedback about what they generally liked or did not like about the course concept. The collected information was analysed by a qualitative content analysis (coding, categorising and counting of items).

(2) Subsequent to the final in-class session, a group of students were invited to provide their feedback during a round-table discussion. The discussion was externally moderated, in order to enable an objective discussion and feedback process as well as a summary of the group's opinion. Students explained their benefits as well as their concerns about the course concept. The documentation of results was conducted by participatory observation and respective note taking. Collected information was subsequently analysed by a qualitative analysis.

(3) For the appropriate discussion of the research question, hypothesis-centered information had to be collected. Certain indicators for the discussion of the research question were deduced from the underlying theoretical framework and from the derived hypotheses. A specific indicator-based online survey was conducted. The online survey questionnaire included 20 questions mainly dealing with topics such as self-guidance during the online phase, cooperation and active participation, comparison with other course formats, and the concept's impact on individual learning success. In total, the online survey was completed by 89 participants (N=89), which reflect a sample of 61%. Collected information was statistically analysed via SPSS.

(4) An analytical evaluation of examination results, both with and without the implementation of the ICM, was conducted. The evaluation included the calculation of performance key indicators such as average examination grades, median, and average failure rates. Usually, a direct comparison of examination results stemming from different semesters is subject to certain limitations. However, the analysed examinations were directly comparable with respect to structure, scope and level of difficulty.

1.6 Empirical analysis and discussion

1.6.1 Hypothesis 1

The transfer of self-guiding and self-responsibility leads to a more intensive engagement with the learning content compared to traditional teaching approaches.

Based on results revealed by the online survey, the students' average weekly workload for the course during the semester amounted to approximately 2.9 hours. The median workload was 3 hours and the workload for the middle 50% of the participants was between 2 and 4 hours per week. 62% of the survey participants dealt for 3 hours or more with the learning materials provided. Furthermore, 76% estimated that their learning activities were more extensive than for other lecture formats.

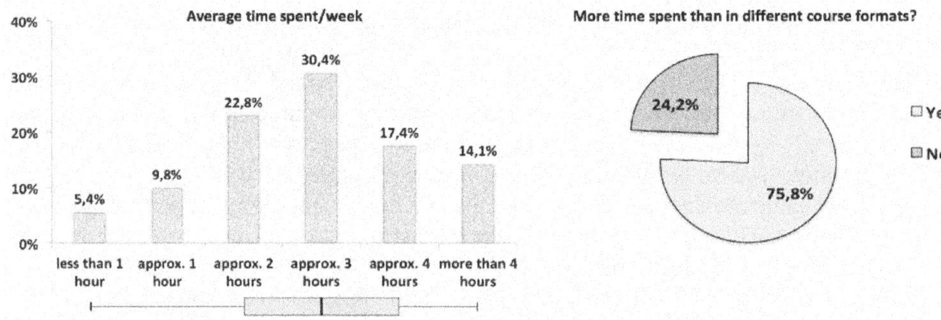

Figure 1.2: Estimation of own workload for the course

According to the collected information, the average workload of students amounted to 66 hours for the semester. This is largely in line with the suggested reference-workload for a 2.5 ECTS credit points course (30 h per credit point). However, based on other studies, it can be assumed that students' workloads are regularly (far) below ECTS suggestions (Loviscach, 2012: 26; Schulmeister/Metzger, 2011). Therefore, the findings indicate that the student's engagement in this course was more intensive than in other traditional teaching formats. However, for the discussion of the hypothesis stated above, it is necessary to determine if the intensified engagement occurred due to the self-directed learning processes. In particular, information collected from the analysis of the open questions and the round-table discussion indicates that students perceive the more intensive engagement and time-consuming preparation rather as negative features of the concept. Thus, the more intensive engagement with learning materials might be the result neither of self-directed learning processes nor of intrinsic motivation. The students' intensive engagement could be driven by the students' assumption that the detailed knowledge and repetition of the entire set of provided learning materials is needed for the successful completion of the final examination. Finally, this might again lead to passive learning by rote. Whether the students' learning habits and attitudes need to be changed in order to better serve the purpose of the concept remains a question to be addressed in future research. However, the collection of information also shows that the permanent accessibility of learning materials as well as possibilities of self-guiding (stopping, rewinding, repeating or skipping) are evaluated as positive. Students evaluate features of self-direction as important for an intensified engagement with learning content.

1.6.2 Hypothesis 2

The design of in-class phases leads to intensified active participation as well as to intensified collaboration and cooperative learning activities.

53% of the online survey participants watched the e-learning videos alone whereas 11% watched the videos together with other students. This might indicate that the cooperation between students is of no significance during the online phase. However, the implementation of the ICM should particularly increase the students' cooperation and active engagement in class. In total, 58% of the online survey participants estimated that their own active involvement during the in-class time had been more intensive due to their previous preparation via e-learning videos. The graphic below shows that the students' estimation of their own active participation in class is broadly balanced. Furthermore, the graphic also shows that the active participation in class of the other students is estimated as more active compared to other course formats by a majority of 52%.

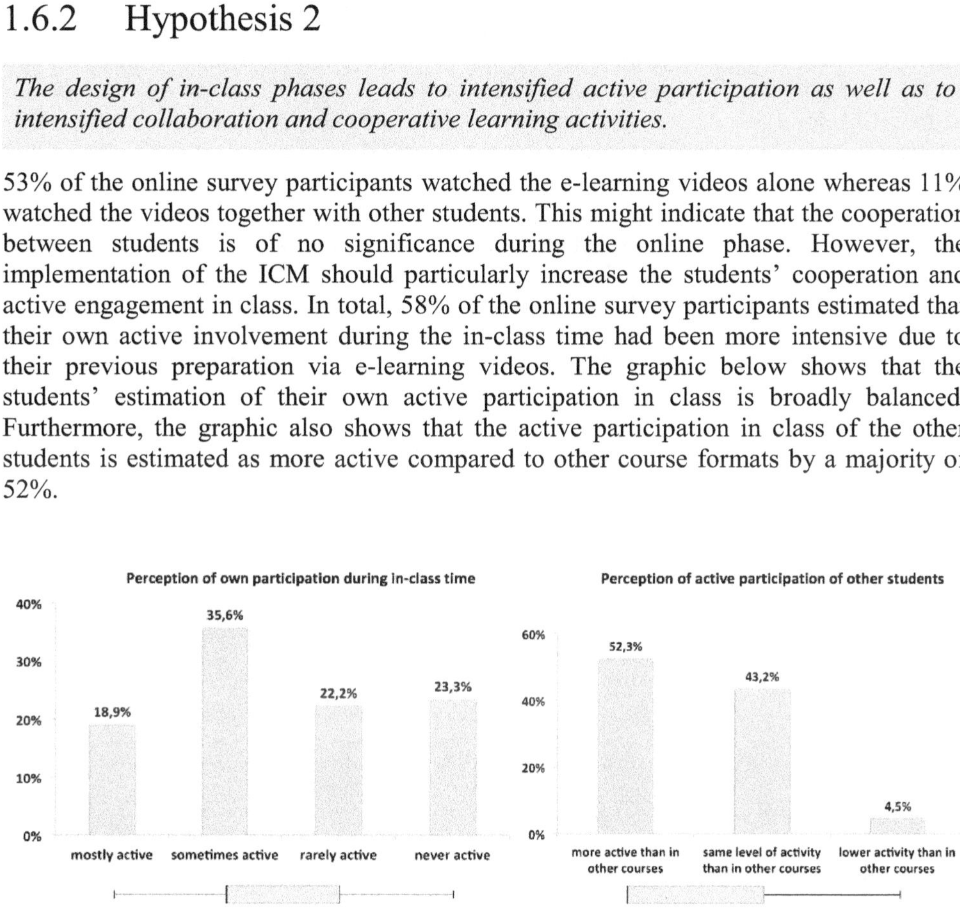

Figure 1.3: Perception of active participation

Empirical information collected from the round-table discussion also indicates that the students appreciate the active cooperation and collaboration in the course. As a result from the analysis, it can be concluded that the increase of active participation, cooperation and collaboration does not only depend on the respective course concept. Additionally, the didactical and methodical design of the course is important to achieve the respective objectives. For this course, it can be stated that on the one hand the active participation is indeed higher than in other course formats, and on the other hand a further increase of active involvement might be realised by enhancing the variety of methods during the in-class phases.

1.6.3 Hypothesis 3

Students intensifying their active involvement or achieving a better understanding of contents prefer the concept compared to traditional teaching approaches.

According to the results collected from the online survey, a 58% majority of the participants would appreciate the implementation of the course concept for other lecture modules. 65% of the participants would retrospectively opt again for the implementation of the ICM for their already completed 'Finance' course in summer semester 2013. Therefore, it can be stated that students prefer the ICM concept compared to traditional lecture formats. The main argument against the implementation was the more extensive workload during online phases. Students partly stated that they would face time constraints for the preparation of in-class time if more than one course is based on an ICM within a given semester. Therefore, the reduction of general engagement in other courses would be necessary. In order to refine the results, it was further analysed if dependence between the general evaluation of the ICM implementation and other collected information could be validated. The charts below present the results.

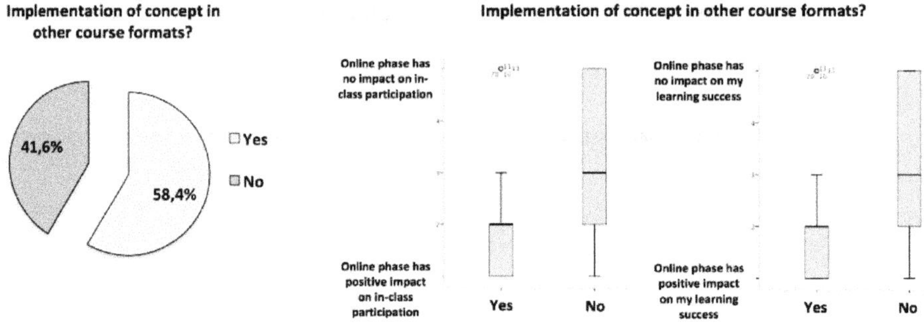

Figure 1.4: Appraisal of the course concept implementation for other lecture modules

In particular, students preferring the implementation of the concept for other lecture modules were able to improve their active participation in class. Furthermore, students who were able to improve the understanding of contents also approved the ICM implementation for other lecture modules. With regard to the implementation of the ICM in summer semester 2013, it can be stated that students prefer this concept. Other academic educators generated comparable results for their respective courses (Braun et al., 2012; Spannagel, 2012: 80).

1.6.4 Hypothesis 4

The implementation of an ICM leads to increased learning success, which may range from a better understanding of the learning contents to better average examination results.

65% of the participants in the online survey estimate that, compared to other learning formats, the ICM-concept improves learning success. 66% of the participants estimate that their understanding of the learning content is generally better due to more extensive preparation during online phases and accordingly more intensive engagement in class. Furthermore, one result from the round-table discussion was that students identified the preparation with e-learning videos and the subsequent active engagement and application of knowledge in class as main drivers for their better understanding of learning content. However, the results reflect the students' subjective impressions and therefore need to be analysed in further detail. The following discussion is mainly based on information derived from the analytical comparison of examination grades. According to this comparison, examination grades during the summer semester 2013 with ICM were considerably better than average grades during the previous three semesters with traditional teaching approaches. Average grade is 2.8 (before: 3.6), median is 2.7 (before: 3.7) and failure rate is 13% (before: 34%) on a scale ranging from 1.0 (very good) to 5.0 (fail). The chart below presents the distribution of grades and the development of failure rates for the observed period.

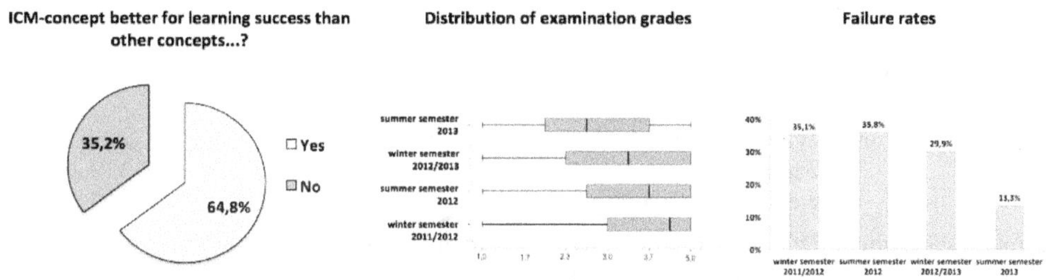

Figure 1.5: Impact on learning success and examination results

Generally, results improved within the observed period (winter semester 2011/2012 to summer semester 2013). It should be pointed out, however, that the results of summer semester 2013 with ICM are significantly better than of the earlier periods. Comparable results for academic education institutions were also identified by other research projects (Moeller, 2013; Loviscach, 2012: 35). The distribution of grades is relatively uniformly distributed within the summer semester 2013. Reasons for the improvements might be the identified more intensive and active engagement and the consequent improvement in understanding of learning content.

1.6.5 Conclusion

Based on the empirical analysis undertaken in the summer semester of 2013, it can be stated that the implementation of the ICM at the HAW Hamburg resulted in a higher learning success than the previously implemented traditional course format. The results indicate that the ICM is accompanied by the enhancement of learner-centered self-guidance and active participation and collaboration within the learning processes.

1.7 Critical acclaim and outlook

The results and conclusions derived from empirical analyses have to be critically reflected regarding certain limitations. Essential empirical data result from the online survey with a sample of N=89 (61%). For 81% of the participants, it was their first attempt at passing the examination; that means students not having passed the examination during prior semesters with high average failure rates are not representatively reflected or determined in the survey. The used data reflect findings from a survey of only one cohort (145 students) in summer semester 2013. More reliable data should be collected in a regularly recurring way.

For the continuous development of the course, it is intended to include certain methodical and didactical changes based on the findings of the research project. The variety of activating methods during the in-class time should be enhanced. Furthermore, the technical advancement of the e-learning videos (mobile access) and the introduction of online tutorials are considered. Finally, the research on the development of adequate examination formats better suitable for the concept of the course remains a major issue.

1.8 References

Bishop, Jacob Lowell/Verleger, Dr. Matthew A. 2013. The flipped classroom: A survey of the research. In: 120th ASEE annual conference & exposition 6/2013. American Society for Engineering Education.

Braun, Isabel/Ritter, Stefan/Vasko, Mikko. 2012. Inverted Classroom - die Vorlesung auf den Kopf gestellt. In: DNH - Die Neue Hochschule, Heft 5. 166–169.

Davis, Christine. 2013. Flipped or inverted learning: Strategies for course design. In: Smyth/ Volker (eds.).l Enhancing Instruction with Visual Media: Utilizing Video and Lecture Capture. Hershey, PA: IGI Global. 241–265.

Friedrich, Helmut F./Mandl, Heinz. 1997. Analyse und Förderung selbstgesteuerten Lernens. In Weinert, Franz E./Mandl, Heinz (eds.). Psychologie der Erwachsenenbildung, Enzyklopädie der Psychologie. Pädagogische Psychologie Bd 4. Göttingen: Hogrefe. 237–293.

Handke, Jürgen/Schäfer, Anna Maria 2012. E-Learning, E-Teaching und E-Assessment in der Hochschullehre. München: Oldenbourg.

Loviscach, Jörn. 2012. Videoerstellung für und Erfahrungen mit dem ICM. In: Handke, Jürgen /Sperl, Alexander (eds.). Das Inverted Classroom Model. Begleitband zur ersten deutschen ICM-Konferenz. München: Oldenbourg. 25–37.

Loviscach, Jörn. 2013. The Inverted Classroom: Where to Go from Here. In: Handke, Jürgen/ Kiesler, Natalie/Wiemeyer, Leonie (eds.). The Inverted Classroom Model. The 2nd German ICM-Conference – Proceedings. Muenchen: Oldenbourg. 3–14.

Lyman, Frank. 1981. The Responsive Classroom Discussion: The Inclusion of All Students. In: Mainstreaming Digest. University of Maryland, College Park, MD. 109–113.

Moeller, Clemens. 2013. Aktivierung in der Studieneingangsphase. Presentation at the Inverted Classroom Conference 2013, Philipps Universität Marburg, Germany. 27/02/2013 http://invertedclassroom.wordpress.com/konferenz2013; accessed on 15/08/2013.

Schäfer, Anna Maria 2012. Das Inverted Classroom Model. In: Handke, Jürgen/Sperl, Alexander (eds.). Das Inverted Classroom Model. Begleitband zur ersten deutschen ICM-Konferenz. München: Oldenbourg. 3–11.

Schulmeister, Rolf/Metzger, Christiane. 2011. Die Workload im Bachelor: Zeitbudget und Studierverhalten. Eine empirische Studie. Münster: Waxmann.

Spannagel, Christian. 2011. Das aktive Plenum in Mathematikvorlesungen. In: Berger, Lutz/Spannagel, Christian/Grzega, Joachim (eds.). Lernen durch Lehren im Fokus. Berichte von LdL-Einsteigern und LdL-Experten. Berlin: epubli. 97–104.

Spannagel, Christian. 2012. Selbstverantwortliches Lernen in der umgedrehten Mathematikvorlesung. In: Handke, Jürgen/Sperl, Alexander (eds.). Das Inverted Classroom Model. Begleitband zur ersten deutschen ICM-Konferenz. München: Oldenbourg. 73–81.

2 The *Inverted Classroom Mastery Model* – A Diary Study

Jürgen Handke

The *Inverted Classroom Model* (ICM) in its basic form swaps the two central activities of teaching and learning. A digital initial phase of content delivery and content acquisition is followed by an in-class phase. In his contribution to the conference volume 2013, Handke discussed a fundamental modification to this basic model, the Inverted Classroom *Mastery* Model (ICMM) and provided first impressionistic judgments.

Now, one year later, he can present a wealth of data that not only confirms the initial judgments but also suggest several beneficiary effects, such as student involvement, 'mastery learning' and in-class participation.

The data was collected in two large on-campus classes, which are obligatory parts of the teacher degree program at Marburg University, and in a Massive Open Online Course that served several hundreds of participants from more than 70 nations.

2.1 Introduction

For eight years we have been experimenting with the *Inverted Classroom* scenario, for almost three years we have written more or less theoretical treatments about the advantages and disadvantages of this teaching and learning model. And we were convinced that our approach would not only be an effective way of integrating digital teaching and learning materials into our classes but we also believed that our students would benefit from this model. However, everything we did during these years was speculative, was based on impressionistic assessments and on our own subjective judgments and those of our students. In October 2013, however, the situation changed. Two generations of high-school finishers filled our lecture halls and had to be served with introductory classes in linguistics. This gave us the wonderful opportunity to not only apply our special, meanwhile price-winning *Inverted Classroom Model* in its 'Mastery' variant but it also provided us with data about general student behavior, in-class attendance and learning success.

Based on two on-campus classes, an introductory class for first-term students during winter 2013/14, and a follow-up class during spring 2014, plus a Massive Open Online Course (MOOC) during spring 2014, we can now present the data that shows the enormous success of the *Inverted Classroom Model* and its application to different course formats. Table 2.1 lists the classes and their main parameters.

Table 2.1: The classes of this study

Class	Type	#Registrations	#Active Participants		#Certificate (Graded)	
Introduction to Linguistics	On-Campus	245	226	92.2 %	184	75.1 %
Morphology and Syntax	On-Campus	106	92	86.8 %	92	86.8 %
The Structure of English	MOOC	530	367	69.2 %	115	21.7 %

2.2 The *Inverted Classroom Mastery Model* (ICMM)

All three classes on which our diary study was based used the *Inverted Classroom Mastery Model*, henceforth abbreviated as ICMM. The principles of the ICMM were introduced in Handke (2013a:16/17) and need not be discussed in detail anymore. In short, each class consists of 10 to 14 units where each unit has an initial online phase of content delivery and content acquisition, a formative test, and a subsequent in-class phase which is replaced by extensive online practical material in the case of the MOOC. Figure 2.1 exhibits the schematic structure of an ICMM-unit for on-campus classes; the MOOC-variant is shown in Figure 2.4.

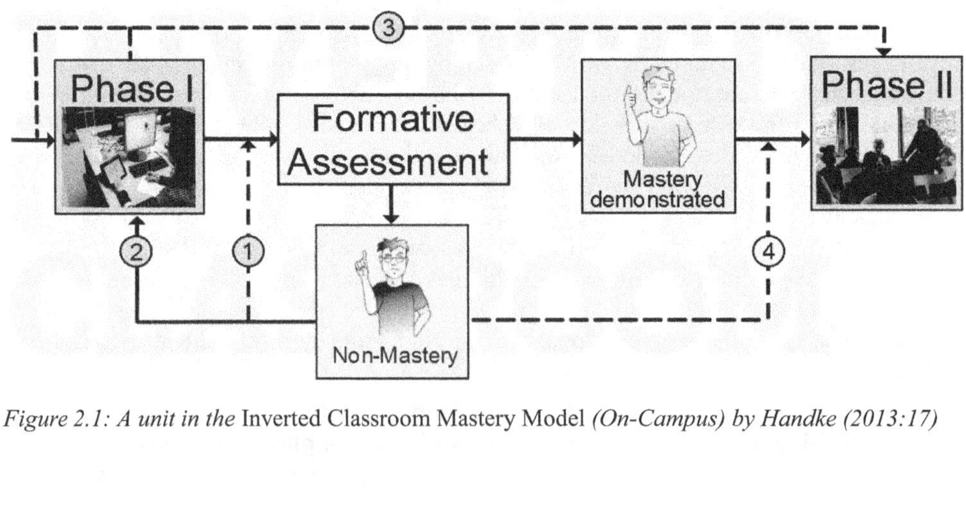

Figure 2.1: A unit in the Inverted Classroom Mastery Model *(On-Campus) by Handke (2013:17)*

Between phase I, the self-guided phase of content acquisition, and phase II, the in-class phase, the formative electronic test allows the students to show mastery. The percentage of the class participants who succeed in doing so prior to the respective in-class meeting is referred to as the 'mastery level'. This level is reached if at least 60% of the questions or more have been answered correctly. In doing so, students have an unlimited number of attempts (path 1, in Figure 2.1), and can – of course – always recur to the first phase of content delivery (2). Yet some students may prefer not to redo the test and join the in-class meeting without having shown mastery (3), and again others may not bother about the mastery tests at all (4). Fortunately, as we will see below, the percentage of 'non-mastery' students in our scenario is relatively low.

All three classes that were part of this study were offered via the *Virtual Linguistics Campus* (VLC), the e-education platform of the conference organizers. The VLC has been operational for more than 15 years and integrates all necessary components for the ICMM (Handke, 2006).

2.2.1 Phase I – Content delivery and content acquisition

A central principle – and probably one reason for the long-lasting success of the *Virtual Linguistics Campus* – lies in the clear structure and the common format of the digital learning units that serve as the backbone for the phase of content delivery and content acquisition in the ICMM. Figure 2.2 exhibits the central structure of such a unit.

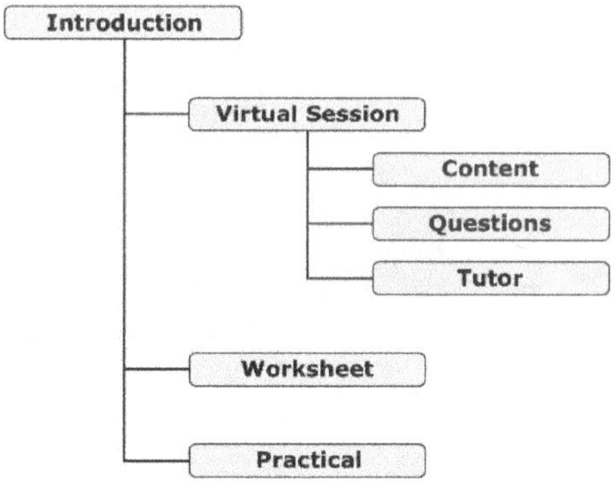

Figure 2.2: Digital content delivery on the VLC

Each unit consists of three parts:

- the *Virtual Session*
  the content of a unit, in the case of the VLC: a combination of multimedia plus e-lectures that can also be accessed independently via YouTube.
- the *Worksheet*
  the formative test (see Figure 2.1) with which class participants can demonstrate mastery.
- the *Practical*
  a collection of tasks and problems to be solved in class

This subdivision is reflected in the navigation menu on the unit start site ('Introduction') where the goals and the central topics of a unit (which also includes specified bibliographical references) are defined. Even though all units adhere to this structure, they can be used and activated along different lines:

- Encapsulated: each unit can be accessed independently
- Sequential: each unit builds upon its predecessor
- Restricted: each unit is available for a limited period

Thus, depending on the class format and the material to be taught, the VLC offers several variants of unit activation.

2.2.2 Phase II – On-Campus

The primary purpose of phase II in an on-campus setting is deepening and practicing. Using the practical questions (see Figure 2.2 'Practical') and additional exercise material which is presented in-class, the students of an on-campus ICMM-class can be taken care of individually. They can ask questions, they solve tasks, and, if suitable, even play games. In accordance with Alison King's (1993) principle *"From sage on stage to Guide on the Side"*, the class instructor no longer teaches in a frontal fashion but joins the students in their tasks: he takes care of them individually or looks after their work in groups. In large groups, such as the classes used for this diary study, the class instructor is supported by postgraduate student tutors who are on par with the class instructor. Figure 2.3 provides a snapshot of this highly intensive style of coaching where the tutors can hardly be distinguished from the students anymore.

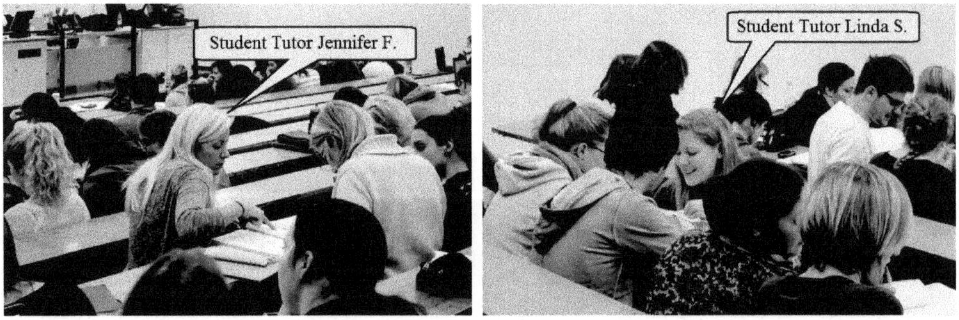

Figure 2.3: Tutoring in phase II of the ICMM

2.2.3 Phase II – MOOC

By definition, a MOOC has no in-class phase. However, this does not mean, that we can totally give up phase II, the phase where in on-campus classes intensive practicing, vivid discussions and individual tutoring take place. As an alternative, we provide the participants of a MOOC with a wealth of multimedial exercise material and a large number of help options, such as model solutions, tooltips, and additional information links – thus, a variety of options where the computer takes over the role of the in-class tutor. For this reason, we have to readjust the model presented in Figure 2.1: phase II is now totally digital and the formative test between phase I and phase II has become summative since its result normally no longer influences the procedures of phase II.

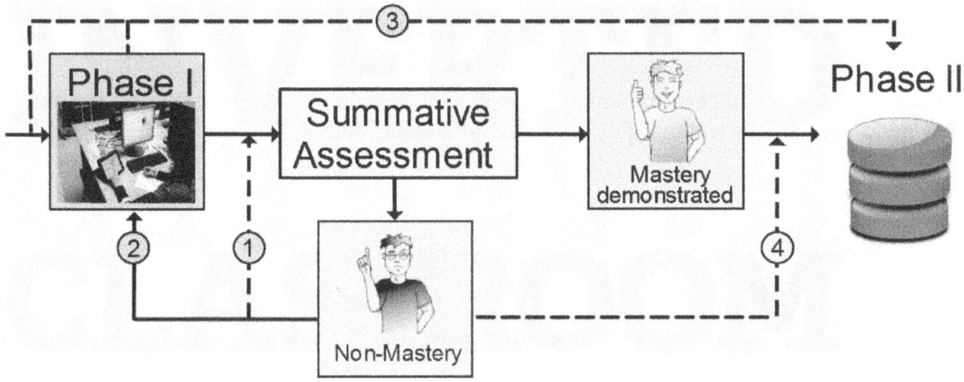

Figure 2.4: A unit in the Inverted Classroom Mastery Model *(MOOC)*

Recently, we have started integrating a 'learner analytics' parameter which correlates the type of exercise material to be given to a participant with his unit-specific mastery level. As pointed out in Handke/Franke (2013:155), this value can be used to select the subsequent practical material, i.e. a first approach to adaptive learning in online classes.

2.3 Evaluation – The diary study

In Table 2.1 we listed the classes that were part of this study and provided an overview of their participants. Yet, the participants who attended these classes were different.

Figure 2.5: On-campus: The Digital Natives are here! A snapshot from the introductory class of winter 2013/14

The students who began their studies in October 2013 clearly belong to a new group of young adults. They have grown up with digital mobile devices such as smart phone and tablet-PC and they have been using the internet for their purposes for several years. Figure 2.5 is a snapshot from the first in-class meeting of the 'Introduction to Linguistics' class in winter 2013/14 where the students were asked to show their digital devices in class.

So the students of the two on-campus classes that became part of this study constitute a new generation of students: highly versatile with technology – the "digital natives".

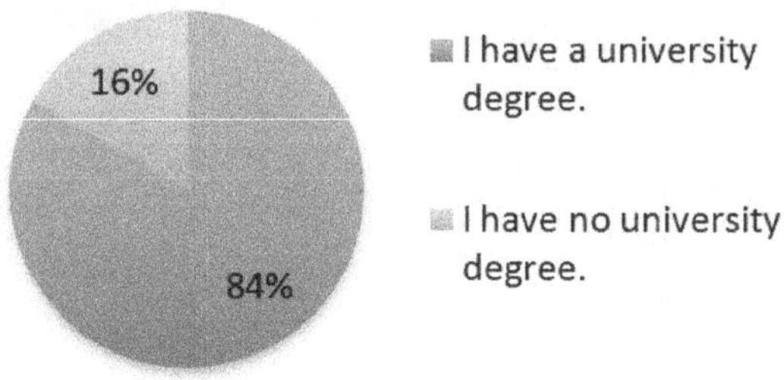

Figure 2.6: The MOOC-Participants

The MOOC-participants, by contrast, did not belong to this generation. They were much older and the majority of them also already had an academic degree.

Despite these age and generation differences, neither of the groups had any problems with the ICMM-realization on the *Virtual Linguistics Campus*. Questions about how to use the digital material or how to submit the worksheets did not occur.

2.3.1 Winter Term 2013/14: *Introduction to Linguistics*

On 7 October 2013, two weeks before term start, 245 students had registered for the class 'Introduction to Linguistics' via the campus management system of Marburg University. Of them, 19 neither showed any online activity nor did they ever attend an in-class meeting. They had registered but never attended the class. So the actual figure of students who eventually were part of the class was 226.

2.3.1.1 Preliminaries

In the *Inverted Classroom* scenario there is no opening or organizational in-class meeting, no special introduction and no class overview. This means that all in-class meetings can almost entirely be dedicated to discussion, practicing, deepening, etc. To familiarize all students with this situation they were given access to the digital components of the class a week before class start. Their only instructions were to watch the class description video (see Handke, 2013b: 62) and to check their computer systems by means of the various options within the class preliminary unit. These instructions were forwarded to them via e-mail:

Dear Class-Participants,

Your "Introduction to Linguistics" class is now active. This means that you can see the main information links including the video about how the class is organized: link: "Description (Video)".

Our first in-class meeting will be next Friday. In the meantime ...

- *study the class preliminaries, and*
- *do the worksheet submission test in the virtual session of the class preliminaries to find out whether your computer settings are in accordance with our requirements!!*

You will receive a notification if everything is fine when you submit the mock worksheet!

Your Class Instructor

In fact, 165 of the 226 participants followed the instructions in this mail and accessed the class preliminaries. The total number of unit activities, i.e. accesses to the individual sites/screens of this preliminary unit before class start was 405.

2.3.1.2 The first unit

Three days before the first in-class meeting, the class participants received a second mail and were asked to go through the digital content of the first content unit 'Language and Linguistics':[1]

Dear Class-Participants,

In your class, you now have access to all units and to all information links (including the video about how the class is organized, framed red on the image attached.) Unless you have already done it go through the "Class Preliminaries" to find out whether your computer is configured correctly and to see how our teaching concept works.

And then, go through the first content unit "Language and Linguistics". I expect you to have worked through this unit by next Friday. This means: Go through the Virtual Session, then do the worksheet (if you fail you can do it again until you pass it!), and finally look at the practical questions (we will discuss them in class). Like all our content units, the unit "Language and Linguistics" contains an E-Lecture (a video which is also available on YouTube).

In other words, prepare well for our first in-class meeting.

Your Class Instructor

After this second mail, whose content was also posted into the first-term students' new *Facebook* group by the student tutors, online activities rose to 2,767 and the number of students who accessed the class was now 201. And of those, 124 students could show mastery: They successfully passed the first worksheet which was a simple multiple-choice test where of 20 questions at least 12 had to be answered correctly. So the mastery level prior to the first in-class meeting was 62%. By the way, the average score for each worksheet was around 90%. Thus, on average, the students answered 18 of the 20 questions correctly. Knowing these figures, which class instructors on the VLC can retrieve via mouse click, the first in-class meeting took place.

It was attended by 162 students, 39 less than those who showed online activities beforehand. So the assumption prior to the in-class meeting was that the mastery level was probably even higher than 62% (those who were not part of the first in-class meeting probably had their reasons ...).

[1] The period between their arrival at their university and term start is especially short for first-term students. Whereas for all other students classes can be activated several weeks before term start, this period is often reduced to less than a week for first-term students.

The in-class meeting itself could now use many of the advantages of the *Inverted Classroom*. After a very brief introductory phase of less than 15 minutes, where the instructor and the tutors introduced themselves, the main points of the digital content were summarized (to serve those who could not show mastery). The remaining 75 minutes were then dedicated to the tasks on the practical sheet and to individual questions. The class instructor and three student tutors went through the lecture hall and assisted the in-class participants in solving their tasks or answered their questions (see Figure 2.3). Students who were felt to have mastered the standard tasks on the practical sheet were given additional tasks and those who seemed to have problems received individual help.

2.3.1.3 Participation and mastery

During the entire class, online activities remained on a high level but in-class participation, which in all our classes is entirely optional, was considerably lower. In week five, the students had to officially confirm their class membership in order to be eligible for the final exam. This led to a drop of the actual number of class participants from 226 to 215. Figure 2.7 exhibits theses participation values for each unit of the introductory class and correlates them with the number of mastery worksheets.

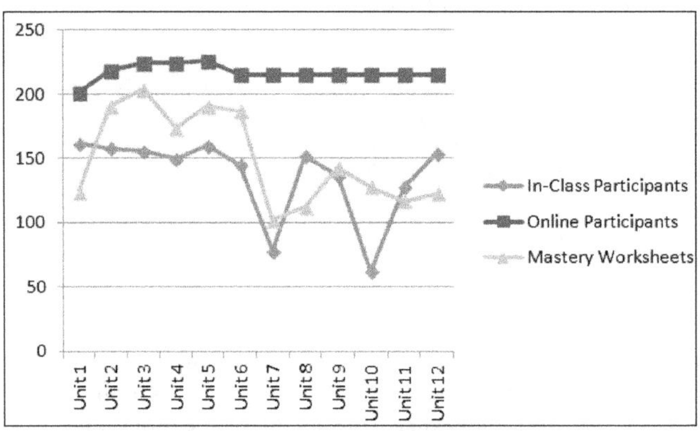

Figure 2.7: Participation and mastery

In the majority of the units, the number of mastery worksheets submitted was higher than the number of in-class participants, this means that the instructor could assume almost 100% mastery in class. In fact, those units where this was not the case, were either extremely complex (unit 8: Syntax) or they were class-flanking: the initial unit, where some participants may still have had problems with the new and unknown teaching and learning scenario, and the final two units where the preparation for the e-exam, and thus a general repetition was the focus rather than the units themselves.

Two units were affected by external factors which could neither be influenced by the teaching model nor by the class instructor and the tutors. Unit 7 was affected by the faculty's reading week where most students stayed at home and unit 10 fell on the last day before the Christmas break so that many students preferred traveling home rather than spending their time on a cold Friday morning at 8 o'clock doing linguistics. Nevertheless more than 30% of the class participants attended the in-class meetings even on these two occasions and the online activities were as high as ever. Thus the average values for in-class attendance as shown in Table 2.2 have to be taken with care.

Table 2.2: Participation and mastery (Averages)

	Before week 5		After week 5	
	#n	Percent	#n	Percent
In-Class Participants	157.2	69.5 %	122.3	56.9 %
Online Participants	218.6	96.7 %	215.0	100 %
Worksheets	949	83.9 %	1736	115 %
Mastery Worksheets	176.8	78.2 %	130.3	60.6 %

Interestingly, the mastery level had dropped from 78% to 60% after week five. Online participation, by contrast, rose to 100%, i.e. all 215 students were permanently active, and the number of worksheets that were submitted after week five even rose to 115%. At first sight, this seems to be a total mismatch: more activities in general but a lower mastery level per unit. However, if we incorporate the submission dates of each individual worksheet and correlate them to their unit activation times, we find that many students after week five no longer adhered to the predefined class rhythm (one unit per week) but submitted a number of worksheets in advance. In other words, they did their work but not in accordance with our expectations – they worked ahead. So they did show mastery but too early. Whether this anticipatory strategy influenced their in-class behavior, i.e. whether they remembered the content or not, was not part of this study.

2.3.1.4 Final results

Two average results deserve special mention:

a) Worksheet Activities

Over the entire class span 2,685 mastery worksheets were submitted, which means that each student statistically submitted 11.9 of the maximally possible 12 worksheets, a superb result. Not all of these worksheets, however, were 'mastery worksheets', i.e. worksheets that were submitted prior to the respective in-class meeting. Here, the average value was 7.9. That is, almost 8 of the 12 worksheets were real mastery worksheets. Thus, the average mastery level of the class was 66.2%: Of all students who showed online activities more than 66% were well prepared prior to the respective in-class meetings.

b) Unit Activities

The average number of unit activities, i.e. the number of websites that were accessed per unit was 1,914. Figure 2.8 shows the development of the unit activities for the entire class.

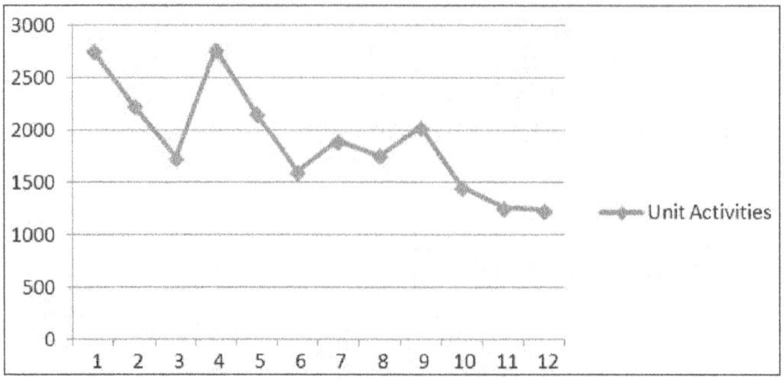

Figure 2.8: Unit activities

Even though the unit activity values dropped towards the end of term (probably because the participants also had to focus on other classes and their final exams), an average value of eight accesses per unit and participant showed the high degree of motivation until the very end of the class.

2.3.1.5 Exams and grading

The class grade2 was calculated on the basis of an electronic exam (e-exam). It consisted of several subtests (input task, multiple choice, phonetic transcription task, word-segmentation, word-selection, counting task), and lasted 120 minutes.

Table 2.3: Exam statistics

Participants	Did not take part	Fail	Pass	Average Grade
215	13	26	176	7.9

Of the 215 participants who registered for the final exams in week five, 202 eventually took part and 176 passed. 13 students dropped out and thus accepted a wanted failure in order to gain time to prepare for the resit-exams. Together with some of those students who failed the exams, they took the resit-exams two months later, and 8 of them passed. Thus, a total of 184 students eventually passed the 'Introduction to Linguistics' module, i.e. a drop-out rate of 14.4 %. Table 2.4 provides an overview of the respective values.

[2] In all classes, grades are assigned on the basis of the 15-point-scale where 15 grade points are the maximum and 0 the minimum. To pass, 5 grade points have to be achieved.

Table 2.4: Class participation and drop-out

Participants	#n	#Drop Out	Percent
initial registrations	245	--	--
online until week 5	226	19	7.7 % of 245
confirmation after week 5	215	11	4.9 % of 226
successful exams	184	31	14.4 % of 215

An interesting fact
The e-exam of the introductory class was offered as a diagnostic test to a group of 45 students who were preparing for the final teacher degree exams two months later. 43 failed and only two students passed it. This may be taken as an indicator for the high difficulty level of the exam since students who are in the middle of their final exam preparation should be expected to pass an introductory exam.

2.3.1.6 Student opinions

One week before class end we asked our students to answer three questions using the Promethean ActiVote student response system:

Question 1: *Compared with other teaching scenarios, in the Inverted Classroom ...*

Option	Answer	Chosen by
A	*I have to work much harder.*	28 %
B	*I have to work harder.*	29 %
C	*I have to invest the same amount of work.*	36 %
D	*I have to work less.*	3 %
E	*I have to work much less.*	5 %

Question 2: *Compared with other teaching scenarios, in the Inverted Classroom ...*

Option	Answer	Chosen by
A	*I learn much more.*	22 %
B	*I learn more.*	37 %
C	*I learn the same amount.*	15 %
D	*I learn less.*	19 %
E	*I learn much less.*	7 %

The answers to these first two questions indicate that the vast majority of the students judged that they have to work harder than in a traditional teaching and learning scenario but also felt that they learn more.[3] In order to find out whether these two subjective judgments would influence their 2nd term choice we asked a third question:

---

[3] The number of students who took part in the vote that was carried across two classes was 172.

Question 3: *Your 2nd term class "Morphology and Syntax" will be offered in two formats. Which one do you prefer?*

Option	Answer	Chosen by
A	*the Inverted Classroom format in one large group*	67.15 %
B	*a traditional format in a group with less than 30 students*	32.85 %

The result was astonishing and pretty clear: Despite the fact that our students felt to have had to invest more work, more than two thirds voted for the ICMM.

With this in mind we planned their 2nd term.

2.3.2 Summer term 2014: *Morphology and Syntax*

The 184 students who successfully passed the introductory module during the first term in winter 2013/14 started their 2nd term in April 2014. In their obligatory class 'Morphology and Syntax', they had the choice between 4 groups:

Table 2.5: Options and Groups for 'Morphology and Syntax', summer term 2014

Group	Teaching Format	Day	Time	Max no. of participants
A	Traditional	Tuesday	14 to 16	30
B	Traditional	Wednesday	10 to 12	30
C	Traditional	Wednesday	12 to 14	30
D	ICMM	Thursday	8 to 10	No limit

Reconsidering the vote at the end of their 1st term (see section 2.3.1.6, question 3), 123 students should have registered for group D, which, admittedly, as far its time was concerned, was not very attractive: 8 o'clock is not among the most preferred start times for a seminar. Nevertheless, 106 students registered for group D, i.e. 57.6% of all second-term students.

But who were the students who took their decision for Group D? As pointed out above (section 2.3.1.5), the average grade for the first-term introduction e-exam was 7.9 grade points but as Table 2.6 suggests the first-term average grades of the participants who chose group D was much higher than the average of the students who opted for one of the traditional groups.

Table 2.6: 1st-term grades and group choice

Choice	Teaching Format	#No. of students	Average Grade (1st term)
Group A, B or C	Traditional	78	6.6
Group D	ICMM	106	9.2

The participants who chose group D were almost 3 grade-points better in their 1st-term exam than the students who chose one of the 'traditional' groups. Why was this so?

Considering the fact that the ICMM supports a more independent learning style where students organize their learning activities themselves, it is not surprising that such a scenario is preferred by the majority of the 'digital natives'. Online activities, the use of mobile devices, the integration of technology in their learning process are almost natural habits to them. Why should they go back to a traditional setting?

An alternative interpretation, however, could be that all those students who did not score well in their 1st term simply wanted to return to a traditional format in order to achieve higher grades.

In any case, assuming that the students who chose group D not only seem to favor the ICMM as such but were also well accustomed to this scenario we could now start without further explanations and instructions in April 2014.

2.3.2.1 Preliminaries

As already mentioned, 106 students registered for the ICMM-class. Of them 14 never attended an in-class meeting nor were they ever active online. Later, it became known that some of them only provisionally registered for the class in March 2014 but in the meantime had changed their degree program or had moved to another university.

2.3.2.2 The first unit

The class consisted of 13 units and, as usual in the ICMM-scenario, there was no preliminary organizational in-class meeting. As described in section 2.3.1.1 all registered class participants received a short initial e-mail where the main organizational details were listed. And since all students were now familiar with the ICMM, further explanations were not necessary.

In fact, of the 92 students who eventually turned out to be part of this class, 87 attended the first in-class meeting, and 63 successfully submitted the first mastery worksheet, thus the mastery level of unit 1 was 79%.

2.3.2.3 Participation and mastery

Participation and mastery were almost identical to the values recorded during winter 2013/14 in the introductory class. Again, the number of mastery worksheets was, by and large, higher than the number of in-class participants and in-class participation hovered around 63%. Figure 2.9 exhibits the values for the 'Morphology and Syntax' class.

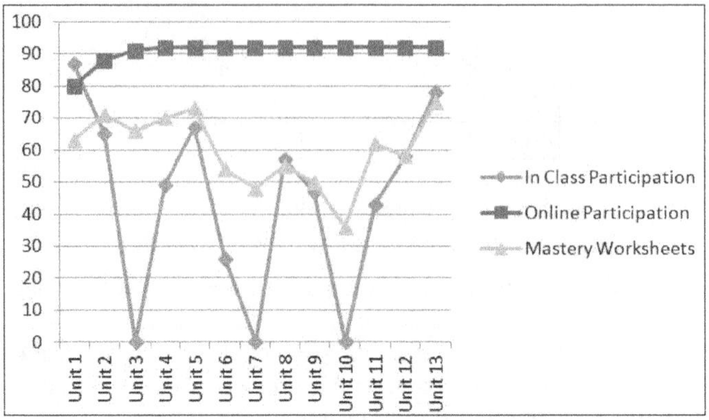

Figure 2.9: Participation (online, in-class) and mastery worksheets

In contrast to the winter-term class 'Introduction to Linguistics', online participation was very high from the start, and all 92 participants confirmed their class participation by week five, thus, there was no drop-out.

Furthermore, all class participants submitted the maximum number of 13 worksheets of which statistically 8.5 were mastery worksheets. Again this means, that at least 66% of all participants attended the respective in-class meetings well prepared. This value could have been higher unless the in-class phases had been affected by three holidays, the 1st of May, Whitsun, and Corpus Christy, and one in-class date that had to be moved to late Friday afternoon (unit 6). As a consequence, the mastery levels for these three units were just around 50%. Obviously, the class participants did not adhere to the weekly rhythm when there were no in-class meetings or the in-class meetings had to be moved.

Table 2.7 presents the respective average values.

*Table 2.7: Participation and mastery (Averages); * = 10 in-class meetings*

	#n	Percent
In-Class Participants*	58	63.0 %
Online Participants	91	98.9 %
Mastery Worksheets	60	66.2 %

The average number of unit activities, i.e. the number of websites that were accessed per unit was 1,043.

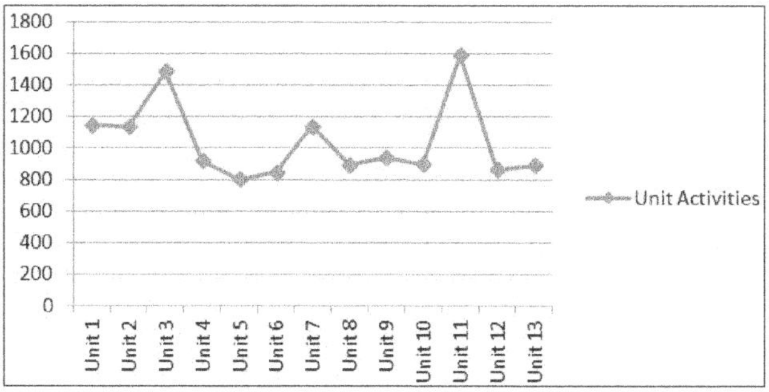

Figure 2.10: Unit activities

The graph in Figure 2.10 exhibits three peaks where the unit activities were considerably above average: Two of them (unit 3 and unit 11) can be attributed to the analysis tasks that were part of these units and whose deadlines coincided with the subsequent in-class phases. Obviously, work on these analysis tasks necessitated a more intensive interaction with the online content.

The peak for unit 7, by contrast, may simply be due to the complexity of the content itself where the topic 'grammar' required more accesses to achieve mastery.

2.3.2.4 Exams and grading

The class grade was calculated on the basis of a 60-minute electronic exam which was taken up by all 92 class participants. They all passed.

Table 2.8: Exam statistics

#Participants	#Did not take part	#Fail	#Pass	Average Grade
92	0	0	92	9.4

The average grade was almost identical with the average the participants achieved in their 1st-term introductory class, a confirmation of the high potential of the students who opted for the ICMM scenario.

2.3.3 Spring 2014: *MOOC Linguistics 201*

In the following, we will compare the data of the two undergraduate on-campus classes with the data generated during our MOOC 'Linguistics 201 – The Structure of English'. This MOOC consisted of 14 units and was accessible over a period of 10 weeks.

The course used the ICMM-format shown in Figure 2.4, i.e. there were of course no in-class meetings and tuition was reduced to a minimum. The instructor's contribution was limited to a total of three round mails and three contributions to the class-related forum.

2.3.3.1 Preliminaries

530 participants took up the MOOC in mid-February 2014. Of them, 163 never accessed the course at all. Even though they were sent the opening mail they never reacted.

Like in the on-campus classes, the opening mail informed all registered participants about the teaching concept, asked them to check their computer system and invited them to explore the details of the VLC concept of online teaching and learning in the 'Class Preliminaries'. Of the 530 registered participants, 238 (44.8 %) followed this invitation. They submitted the mock worksheet and showed a total of 1,046 unit activities.

Like in all VLC-MOOCs, two certificates could be gained:

- the 'statement of accomplishment'
- the 'statement of participation'

To be awarded the 'statement of accomplishment' the participants had to demonstrate their mastery by reaching a class average of 60% or more based on the electronic tests that were associated with each unit. The 'statement of participation', by contrast, was issued for regular online activities and a mastery level between 1 and 59 %.

2.3.3.2 Participation and mastery

As usual for a MOOC, the number of actual participants, i.e. those participants who were permanently active and regularly accessed the digital content was much lower than the number of registrations. Of the 530 registrations, only 341 (64.3 %) were permanently active.[4]

Since there were no in-class meetings, the participants were not obliged to show mastery. If they wanted to obtain a graded statement of accomplishment they had to do the worksheets (one per unit), but they did not have to submit them at a particular time. Nevertheless, and this is perhaps one of the most remarkable results of the MOOC 'Linguistics 201', more than 11% of the participants did show mastery. They took the course like an on-campus class an adhered to the predefined rhythm. Table 2.9 shows these astonishing values.

Table 2.9: Participation and mastery (Averages)

	#n	Percent
Online Participants	341	64.3 %
Mastery Worksheets	63	11.9 %

Whereas the mastery level remained relatively stable throughout the course, online participation rose from 289 (54.5 %) on class start to 365 (68.9 %) at the very end. Figure 2.11 displays these two central MOOC parameters.

4 Compared to the low success rates of the MOOCs offered elsewhere this is still a high value [INT 1].

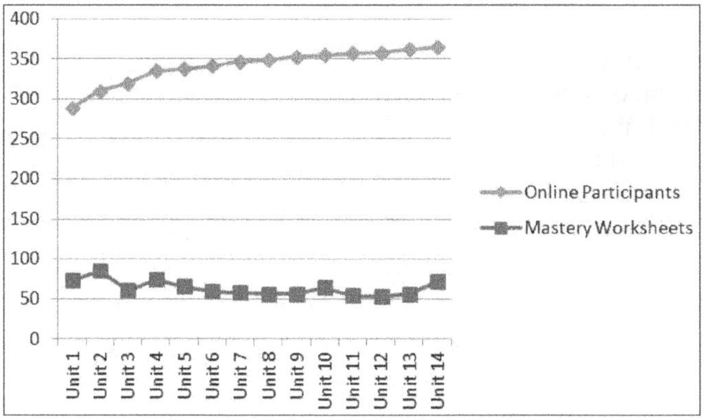

Figure 2.11: Participation (online) and mastery worksheets

Despite the steady increase of online participants, their unit activities dropped considerably. Figure 2.12 displays this tendency.

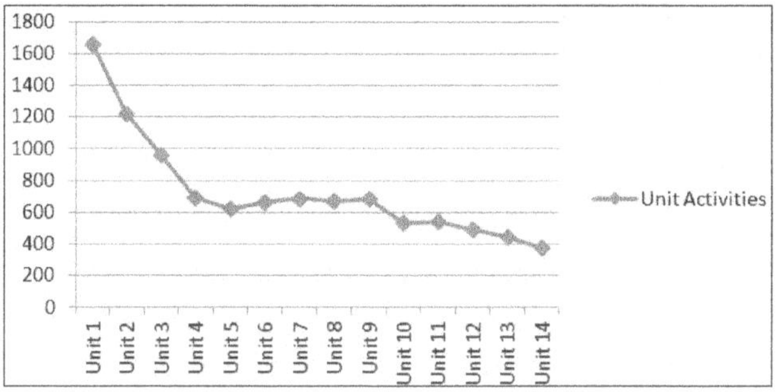

Figure 2.12: Unit activities

Several factors may be used to explain these tendencies which run counter to the development in on-campus classes.

a) MOOCs have no final exam.

   ➢ Without a final exam, intensive repetition towards class end becomes superfluous.

b) MOOCs involve effort

   ➢ The longer a MOOC is running, the more do participants seem to realize that they can hardly keep up their high degree of involvement they showed during the initial stages of the MOOC.

c) High Expectations

   ➢ The big slope between unit 1 and 4 in Figure 2.12 is probably due to a harsh drop of "excitement" when MOOC-participants realize that the content of the MOOC is not what they expected.

d) MOOC certification

- A relatively large number of MOOC-participants may initially have had the intention to meet the conditions for 'a graded statement of accomplishment' where they have to reach a class mastery level of 60% or more. Towards class end, they may have realized that such a certificate had become out of reach and that a 'statement of participation' would be their only option. As a result, they stopped any class activities or at least reduced their involvement to a minimum.
- This trend is reflected by the use of the class-related forum, where the number of activities (contributions and new threads) almost came to a halt towards class end.

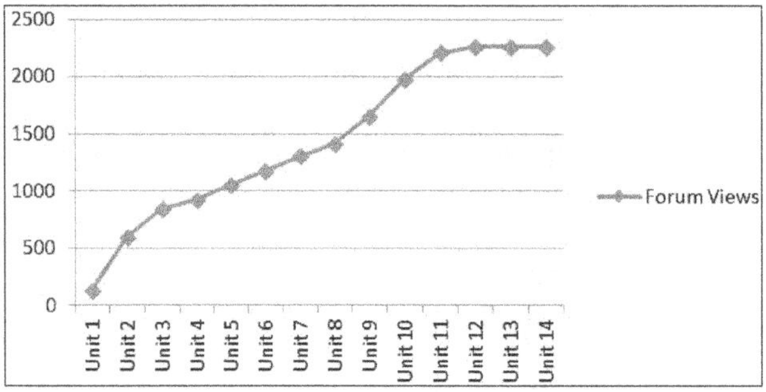

Figure 2.13: Forum activities during MOOC 201

2.3.3.3 Certification

MOOCs do not have a final exam – if they had several problems would have to be solved, among them the authentication problem (how can we guarantee that the participants do not use external help?). Thus, we can only deliver simple statements of participation or mastery certificates, the so-called statements of accomplishment (see section 2.3.3.1). Table 2.10 shows these final MOOC statistics:

Table 2.10: MOOC participation and certification

# Initial Registration	# Active Participation	# Statement of Participation	# Statement of Accomplishment
530	341 (64.3 %)	116 (21.9 %)	115 (21.7 %)

Considering the low accomplishment rates of MOOCs in a global context, these results are extraordinarily high.

2.4 Summary

Even though we have only provided longitudinal data in a diary format in this study we can clearly conclude that for the majority of our students – the new 'digital generation' – the *Inverted Classroom* offers numerous advantages as compared with traditional teaching and learning scenarios. It supports a new learning style where students can use their digital devices without having to change their standard habits. Furthermore, the *Inverted Classroom Model* provides the students with a certain degree of flexibility allowing them to organize themselves and make learning place- and time-independent. However, and this is where *mastery learning* comes in, many students also seem to favor strict rhythms. They need regular testing in a weekly rhythm in order to learn more intensively. That this regularity also plays a role in MOOCs was supported by the data available.

The simple *Inverted Classroom* scenario alone may thus not be sufficient to achieve the desired learning effects. An important factor for the success of the on-campus classes as well as for the relatively high accomplishment rates of the VLC-MOOC seems to lie in the regular option to show mastery. For the participants of an on-campus class, their mastery level seems to be a measure of confidence before the in-class meetings and for the class instructor it is a formative parameter for the organization of the in-class meeting (re-teaching or not?).

So the lesson we learned from this diary study should be clear: The benefits of inverting classes are overwhelming. The scenario is more transparent than a traditional teaching and learning scenario, it can guarantee content delivery (the internet is not affected by any holidays) and it allows all learners to apply their own rhythm. And with cleverly designed in-class phases, that may also involve new aspects of gamification and adaptive elements, we can create higher levels of excitement than in traditional scenarios where content delivery is in the focus and the interaction with the students is often reduced to a minimum.

A minority of students, however, still seems to prefer traditional settings.

Thus, we should make sure not to lose these students who obviously either have general difficulties with this new freedom or who are simply not ready for the inverted classroom with its large number of digital components, yet.

2.5 References

Handke, Jürgen. 2006. The Virtual Linguistics Campus – An Overview. In: Handke, Jürgen/ Franke, Peter (eds.). The Virtual Linguistics Campus – Strategies and Concepts for Successful E-Learning. Münster: Waxmann. 14–36.

Handke, Jürgen. 2013a. Beyond a Simple ICM. In: Handke, Jürgen/Kiesler, Natalie/Wiemeyer, Leonie (eds.). The Inverted Classroom Model. The 2nd German ICM-Conference – Proceedings. München: Oldenbourg Verlag. 15–20.

Handke, Jürgen. 2013b. The VLC Video Strategy. In: Handke, Jürgen/Kiesler, Natalie/Wiemeyer, Leonie (eds.). The Inverted Classroom Model. The 2nd German ICM-Conference – Proceedings. München: Oldenbourg Verlag. 59–76.

Handke, Jürgen/Franke, Peter. 2013. xMOOCs im Virtual Linguistics Campus: Inhalte, Assessment und Mehrwert. In: Schulmeister, Rolf (ed.). Massive Open Online Courses. Münster: Waxmann. 101–126.

King, Alison. 1993. From Sage on the Stage to Guide on the Side. College Teaching, Vol. 41, No. 1. Taylor & Francis Ltd.

[INT 1] Lankau, Rolf. Ohne Dozenten geht es nicht. http://www.zeit.de/2014/03/online-kurse-anti-mooc; last accessed on 20/07/2014.

II Recent Developments

Inspired by the 2014 ICM conference, different adjustments to the *Inverted Classroom Model* have been implemented. They concern content delivery and content acquisition and the following in-class phase. As discussed in the subsequent contributions to this volume, special attention was given to the modification of the organization of the in-class phase.

A new development within the ICMM implementation at Marburg University is the use of student tutors. In the present conference proceedings, this development is analyzed from different perspectives. A description of their role as student tutors within the ICMM linguistics classroom is given by Jennifer Floyd, Anja Penßler-Beyer, Katharina Weber and Mareike Wempen. This first-hand report from active ICMM tutors also focuses on challenges and benefits of this tutoring concept.

With the aim to advance the tutoring concept, toassure the quality as well as to improve the selection process the tutor trainers, Eva-Marie Großkurth und Sabrina Zeaiter report on recent experience with this novel form of implementing tutors in in-class sessions. Tasks, challenges and resulting problems for the ICMM tutors will be outlined in short as they play an important role for the determination of required qualities and methods for the selection process of prospective tutors.

Educational videos are a primary means to deliver content in ICM-based teaching and learning settings. In their article, Kerstin Raudonat and colleagues discuss the importance of providing suitable communication options via digital media during the online phase. The platform *Studystar* which was developed at Heilbronn University enables for coherent dialogues and provides functions for an effective and discourse-oriented use of video material.

3 Student Tutors in ICMM Courses in Academic Teaching: First Experiences

Jennifer Floyd, Anja Penßler-Beyer, Katharina Weber, Mareike Wempen

3.1 The *Inverted Classroom Mastery Model*

Teaching in the 21st century means that every teacher has to deal with the omnipresence of the internet and the rapid expansion of knowledge databases. This is both challenging and of great advantage on all levels of teaching – from primary school up to the university level. Another problem instructors are confronted with is the many individual types of learners they face in their lectures and seminars, as Lage/Platt/Treglia (2000) state:

> *"If an instructor wanted to lecture for those students who learn best via lecturing, conduct experiments for the experiential learner, give group assignments for the collaborative and cooperative learners and oversee self-directed study for the independent learners, then he would need to increase the student contact time fourfold."*(30)

This is where the foundations were laid for the *Inverted Classroom Model* (ICM). In 2002, the Linguistic Engineering Team at the English Department at the University of Marburg came to the same conclusion and implemented the concept of an *Inverted Classroom* to their university courses (Handke/Franke, 2006). The further development, i.e. the introduction of a mastery component followed in 2009 after realizing that a simple ICM does not suit the needs of linguistics courses at university level. Thus the *Inverted Classroom Mastery Model* (ICMM) was established.

Inverting the classroom, however, requires an understanding of what the classroom looks like in a traditional understanding. During a traditional learning scenario both content delivery and content acquisition are provided in class. In a second phase students practice and deepen the knowledge on their own, for example on the basis of additional homework tasks (cf. Schäfer, 2012).

3.2 The two phases of the ICMM

The first phase of the ICMM scenario concerns the content delivery and the content acquisition (cf. Handke, 2014, Chapter 2.2, in this volume). Both take place online, self-guided and prior to the in-class meeting. In phase two, students come to class in order to practice and to deepen what they have learned. This, of course, requires the students to work through the respective online material prior to the respective in-class meeting. The online material is available via the *Virtual Linguistics Campus* (VLC), where the content is supported by means of interactive multimedia features such as animations, different task types, interactive tutors[1], and additional readings. In order for the course instructor to see whether the student acquired and understood the online content of the respective session, an interactive worksheet needs to be mastered and submitted. At least 60% of the given answers must be correct for the results to be stored in the database. If students fail this so-called 'mastery level', they can work through the content repeatedly and redo the worksheet. A short and anonymous poll at the beginning of each in-class meeting serves as a back-up to the instructor. By taking into account the result of the 'entrance test', he or she then decides, whether selected aspects need to be retaught or whether the beneficial phase of active in-class practicing can begin. (cf. Handke, 2014, Chapter 2.2, in this volume)

But is it possible to apply the ICMM to all academic fields universally? Here, Handke and Schäfer propose that the ideal ICM-scenario can be realized in multimedia-supported courses in combination with e-assessment procedures in phase one, i.e. the online phase. However, the ICM only works if the instructor is able to change his role from being a pure knowledge broker into a learning facilitator of the students, accompanying their learning process (Handke/Schäfer, 2012: 118f).

3.3 The role of the tutors in the ICMM

The decision to deploy tutors in the actual in-class scenario can be regarded as an extension to and a further development of the ICMM. Before, the instructor managed the classroom all on his own, thus, he was in charge of content delivery to large groups of students. However, such a scenario cannot account for differentiation within the student body. A university teacher may want to satisfy both the needs of students that acquire knowledge quickly, as well as of those students who need additional guidance. This is more difficult within larger groups of students, especially when a single instructor is in charge.

Tutors aim at multiplying the purview of the instructor in class and beyond. The role of the tutors begins with the revision of pre-existing material and preparation of new content for the virtual session[2]. Since the tutors have access to the virtual sessions

[1] The interactive tutors on the VLC consist of various task types which help the students with keeping track of their learning progress.

[2] The so-called virtual sessions are the online units on the e-learning platform. Within the ICMM model, the content is delivered via these online sessions, supported by interactive exercises and formative tests.

including the practical tasks, e-assessments and solutions, they can check them before they are dealt with in-class. With several pairs of eyes and constant feedback by the students, the quality of the content is more likely to be assured. The tutors need to possess a high level of competency in the course content, since they are expected to be able to answer any questions the students might have (cf. Großkurth/Zeaiter, 2014, in this volume). The weekly tasks for the tutors are exemplified in Table 3.1 below.

Table 3.1: The tutors' tasks

Working Hours	Which phase of the ICMM ?		Tasks
1h	Before the in-class meeting	Meeting with lecturer	Wrapping up the previous in-class meeting Preparation of this week's content
2-4h	During the in-class meeting	In-class meetings	Support students in-class Guide them through exercises
1-2h	After the in-class meeting	Office hours	First point of contact in the need of advice
1-2h	After/before the in-class meeting	Preparing next week's content	Instructions to students via e-mail, slides, exercises

Each in-class meeting was preceded by a consultation with the lecturer. The lecturer informed the tutors about the overall structure of this week's session. He prepared the presentation slides and actual statistics on the students' unit accesses. The tutors resumed on their office hours and received advice on the questions they were not able to solve within their team. Also, multiple choice questions were developed and discussed during the meeting. After the meeting, the tutors transferred the multiple choice questions to the software and set up the technical conditions for the anonymous polls.

Five tutors were assigned to two courses: 'Introduction to Linguistics' and 'Introduction to Phonetics, Phonology, and Transcription'. The two courses are compulsory for undergraduate students in the bachelor degree program as well as in the teacher degree program. The course 'Introduction to Linguistics' was supported by three tutors, and the two classes for the course 'Introduction to Phonetics, Phonology, and Transcription' were supported by two. The tutors had the chance to decide on the topic of their choices and were able to rotate between courses.

All online sessions were already programmed ready-for-use prior to the beginning of the tutors' work. However, they were not static; rather feedback and suggestions for improvement were still taken into account. The tutors are thus directly involved in the preparation of the exercises conducted in-class.

Technological devices supported all in-class phases. In-class sessions started with a 15-minute talk of the lecturer. This talk built upon the online content and provided the students with an overview of the topics the online session dealt with. The instructor's talk was followed by three to five multiple choice questions that revolved around the content of the virtual session. The tutors handed out the electronic voting devices, supervised their usage, and were in charge of the whole scenario, ensuring that it ran smoothly without technical difficulties. The software in use was *ActivInspire* and the audience response system is called *ActiVotes*. Apart from those planned testing scenarios, it is still possible to involve the students by conducting spontaneous quizzes with additional content-related multiple choice questions at any time during the in-class phase. Analyzing the percentage of correct and incorrect answers then helps both the lecturer and the tutors in supporting the students to fill any gaps where necessary.

Content and interactive exercises are accessible one week prior to the in-class session as virtual sessions online. As a result, students can study and practice the content of the upcoming meeting. Ideally, they have already prepared the practicals when they deal with them in-class. Experience has shown that students who do not prepare the online content beforehand have significant problems with doing the exercises during the in-class phase. Usually, the students notice this and – in most cases – adapt their learning pattern to come to class better prepared. Since the in-class meeting of the ICMM builds upon the preparatory content acquisition at home, students who do not do their work are less likely to be successful.

During the in-class meetings, the instructor and the tutors are present to help with problems, to answer questions, and to check the students' solutions. This requires a certain amount of spontaneity so as to move from student to student and help with their individual problems (cf. Großkurth/Zeaiter, 2014, in this volume). The number of students who attended each session varied between 100 up to 250. Prior to and directly after federal holidays numbers were low, whereas from four weeks onwards prior to the exam numbers were high (cf. Handke, 2014, Chapter 2.3, in this volume). Since there is always one lecturer and at least two tutors present, the amount of students is manageable, even if many of the students would like to talk to the instructor or one of the tutors individually. Often it is possible to talk to small groups of students at once. Group work, use of technological devices, and web research was generally encouraged during the in-class sessions.

The general atmosphere is quite open and there are fewer hesitations to talk, but in-class meetings with such an amount of students obviously pose specific problems such as noise and the mobility of the tutors. The latter problem is easily solved with a lecture hall that is equipped with enough seats to leave every few rows free so students can be reached individually. The noise is something both lecturers/tutors and students must come to terms with, but it can even work to the students' advantage, since it creates a sort of barrier beyond which a one-on-one talk with the lecturer or tutor does not carry. Students might therefore feel less exposed than in traditional tutorials. Also, they are offered more chances to talk to the instructor – something which is usually not an option in large-scale lectures.

This guides us to another important advantage for everyone involved in this scenario: the availability of the lecturer. Questions that go beyond the allotted content for the in-class meetings can sometimes not be answered by the tutors right away. These sorts of questions can now be passed on to the present instructor who has the necessary knowledge to help with these problems. Helping the student thus no longer involves postponing to the next session or to an e-mail sometime later that day. Instead, the students' questions can be answered right then and there, while they are most relevant.

Since the coming generations of students are very technology savvy and are used to having access to the web all the time, the students are encouraged to use their tablets or computers in the in-class meetings to search online for answers – all the while supervised by a lecturer or tutor who can check the appropriateness of the findings. It is an advantage if the tutors have tablets with them, e.g. to be able to access the online content again. Compared with the tutors who rely on print-outs as a help, the assistants with an electronic device are better equipped to help the students, since they can not only work with the content of the virtual sessions, but they can also use their tablets as notepads or drawing boards. The resulting notes and sketches are digital, so they can be sent around via e-mail after the in-class session.

3.4 Tutors beyond the classroom

Besides supporting the students by taking part in the in-class meetings, there were additional tasks to fulfill in order to ensure high-quality, well-organized instruction. As every student needed to be registered for the right class according to their course of studies and was required to have full and permanent access to the online content, it was important to react instantly in case any problems occurred. These problems were mostly due to students forgetting their login data or having registered for the wrong course and could be dealt with easily. Each of the tutors was responsible for one of the courses which ensured both an equal amount of work and the possibility to handle every student's questions or problems as soon as possible. The class on phonetics was divided into two groups, as the course content of the bachelor students and those studying on a teaching degree differed at specific points. Thus, one of the tutors who had already acquired a bachelor degree was responsible for the bachelor group and the other students were supported by the tutor studying on a teaching degree herself.

In addition to resolving issues, it was the tutors' task to provide the students with the interactive whiteboard slides that were created during the in-class meetings. Furthermore, tutors were responsible for passing along important information about how to prepare for the following in-class meeting, which things to bring to class, changes of the time or room of the in-class meeting, as well as information concerning the final e-exam. The tutors were able to view the number of unit accesses and submitted worksheets of every student and could thus, if necessary, remind students of the importance of thorough preparation. Furthermore, the tutors were required to verify that each student had provided all the necessary information to be admitted to the final e-exam, such as the student registration number and the necessary amount of successfully completed worksheets. Again, those students who still needed to add missing information could be addressed directly via the tutors' own staff e-mail account.

In addition to the possibility of contacting the tutors via e-mail, the students were also able to ask anything before or after the in-class meetings. In order to provide the possibility of one-to-one advising despite the large number of students, a two-hour office hour was offered for the course 'Introduction to Linguistics' and a one-hour office hour for the course 'Phonetics, Phonology and Transcription.' The office hours were regularly visited by students, particularly prior to or following the deadlines for graded e-assessments and during the weeks directly preceding the final exam. These office hours presented students with the opportunity to ask questions or express criticism outside the classroom. This enabled the tutors to save time during the in-class meetings and to offer each student individualized guidance and advice as necessary.

Not only was it possible to contact the students via e-mail, but also the popularity of social media (in this case *Facebook*) was utilized. A closed *Facebook* group was created for each of the two courses and every participant was informed about the option to participate in these groups. During the course of the semester, 182 members joined the group, many of which participated actively on a regular basis. The advantage of this particular kind of group was that everyone who wanted to become a member needed to send a request to do so. Only members of the groups were able to view the contents of it. This meant that, the instructor, who was not a member of either *Facebook* group, was unable to read the questions or comments by the students. As a result, students could ask any question or express criticism without having to fear any potential consequences. The fact that nearly every student had their own *Facebook* account and checked it regularly made it easy to spread important information quickly. Especially the availability of a mobile application was very helpful. The greatest advantage of this kind of communication was the fact that every member of the group could see the questions of their fellow students and the corresponding responses. This prevented redundant questions, made everyone aware of significant content to consider and, most importantly, enabled the students to support one another. The tutors deliberately waited some time after a question was posted in order to give the other students the chance to answer it. In this manner, many high-quality and well-researched answers were given. These responses and resulting discussions were advantageous for all participants, as Figure 3.1 reveals:

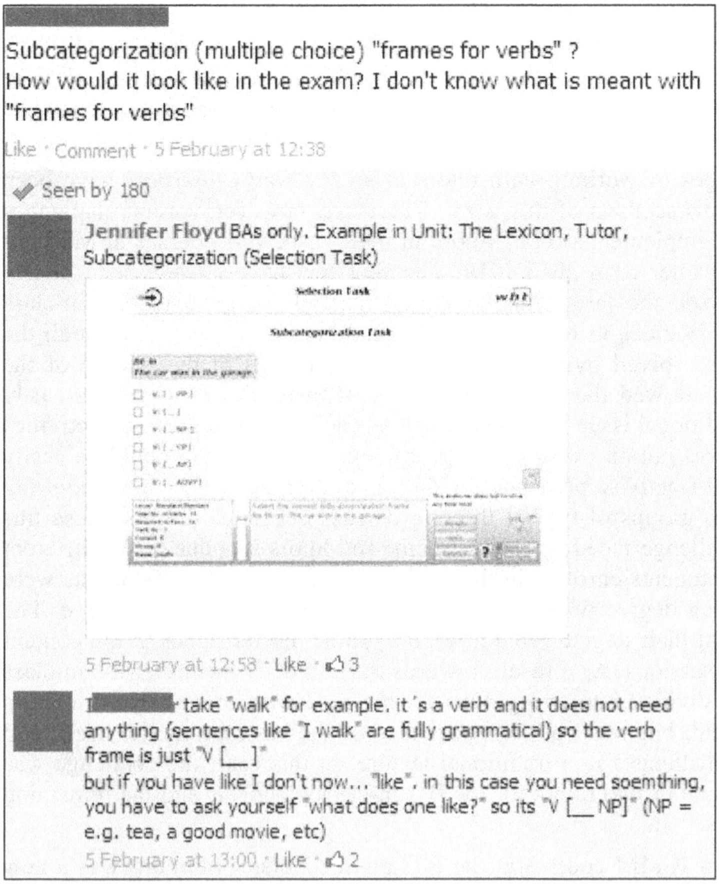

Figure 3.1: Discussion of course content by students and tutors in Facebook group

3.5 Outcomes and consequences

Thus far, an overview of the typical ICMM course has been provided, and the role and tasks of tutors in and outside of the ICMM classroom have been discussed. But what are the benefits and challenges of the implementation of tutors in the ICMM?

In a class following the ICMM, the content acquisition phase completed virtually at home is not a challenge for even very large classes, as this phase is done individually at one's own pace and convenience. The in-class session where content is further discussed and practiced, however, is faced with significant difficulties once the class becomes larger. The more students in a class, the more difficult it is for the instructor to reach each student. The utilization of tutors, therefore, is an alternative method to provide each student with the opportunity to obtain expert input and feedback. As discussed beforehand in the previous sections, group activities can be undertaken during the in-class session with guidance from the tutors and instructor. Moreover, in the rare case that a tutor is unsure of how best to answer a question or explain a concept, the course instructor is always present to clarify any misconceptions or further explain difficult topics. tutors and instructors can additionally work together to provide various takes on the content, offering various tasks, examples, and experiences of topics from the subject at hand – after all, multiple minds are stronger than one.

The numerous advantages of working with tutors in an *Inverted Classroom* have been illustrated in the previous sections of this work. There are, however, certain challenges which arose during the implementation of tutors in the two ICMM courses at Marburg University during the winter term 2013/2014. The first two have already been briefly mentioned and stem from the large number of participants assigned to one in-class meeting. This led to difficulties in reaching each student and in navigating through the participants, which were solved by leaving a few rows of seats in the middle of the lecture halls free. This allowed the instructor and tutors to reach most students easily when necessary. An additional issue was the occasional loudness during certain activities and discussions. This was not an overwhelming problem, however, and could be easily controlled by the type of activity prepared for the class. Normally, activities requiring students to split up into groups of two or three to discuss questions did not cause this issue. An additional challenge faced by the instructor and tutors was due to the different study programs of the students enrolled in the courses. In this case, some students were completing their teaching degree while others were completing a bachelor degree. The different requirements of their degree programs led to some discrepancies in the content presented in the online sessions. As a result, towards the end of the semester the in-class sessions were partially divided into two groups for the separate material. This situation was not necessarily ideal, but was not a consequence of the teaching model itself, and would pose the same challenges in a traditional lecture. In this case, the challenge was dealt with by allotting one or two tutors for the BA in-class practicals and the remaining for the teaching students.

The use of tutors in two ICMM courses at the Philipps University Marburg was a new experience for the instructor, tutors, and students, and the role of the tutors in the courses was developed and modified throughout the semester as new and unexpected challenges arose. Overall, as was confirmed by anonymous student evaluations (cf. Handke, 2014, in this volume), the use of tutors in the courses was very successful and advantageous for the course participants. The majority of students not only appreciated the support they received from the tutors, but also stated that due to the tutors in combination with the instructor, they were able to better understand and master course content. It can thus confidently be concluded that the use of tutors in courses following the ICMM can lead to a more successful course, particularly in the case of those with a large number of participants.

3.6 References

Lage, Maureen J./Platt, Glenn J./Treglia, Michael. 2000. Inverting the classroom: A gateway to creating an inclusive learning environment. The Journal of Economic Education, 31(1), 30–43.

Großkurth, Eva-Marie/Zeaiter, Sabrina. 2014. Tutors in the ICMM: A Way to Professionalized Tutor Selection and Quality Assurance – First Observations. In this volume. 47–61.

Handke, Jürgen/Franke, Peter (eds.). 2006. The Virtual Linguistics Campus – Strategies and Concepts for Successful E-Learning. Münster: Waxmann.

Handke, Jürgen/Schäfer, Anna Maria 2012. E-Learning, E-Teaching und E-Assessment in der Hochschullehre. Eine Anleitung. München: Oldenbourg.

Handke, Jürgen. 2013. Beyond a Simple ICM. In: Handke, Jürgen/Kiesler, Natalie/Wiemeyer, Leonie (eds.). The Inverted Classroom Model. The 2nd German ICM-Conference – Proceedings. München: Oldenbourg Verlag. 15–20.

Handke, Jürgen. 2014. The Inverted Classroom Mastery Model – A Diary Study. In this volume. 15–34.

4 Tutors in the ICMM: A Way to Professionalized Tutor Selection and Quality Assurance – First Observations

Eva-Marie Großkurth & Sabrina Zeaiter

A new development within the ICMM is the use of student tutors. In the present conference proceedings, this development is analyzed from three different perspectives. The preceding article by Jürgen Handke discusses the topic from the perspective of the course instructor and the article by Floyd et al. (in this volume) is a first-hand report from active ICMM tutors. This present article reports on recent experience with this novel form of implementing tutors in in-class sessions. The perspective applied here is that of trainers of tutors with the aim to advance the tutoring concept, assure the quality as well as improve the selection process.

The first part of this present article will briefly introduce the teaching concept used at the Linguistic Department of the Philipps University Marburg. Furthermore, tasks, challenges and resulting problems for the ICMM tutors will be outlined in short (for an in-depth first-hand report cf. Floyd et al., 2014 in this volume). The article concludes with notions about the selection process and quality assurance.

However, before going into details, allow for a few words to define the here used terminology, i.e. tutor. Among the English speaking countries, there is a discrepancy in the use and understanding of the term 'tutor'. While for example universities in the UK, Australia, New Zealand and South Africa as well as some Canadian ones use the term 'tutor', American and Canadian universities refer to the same or similar concept with the term 'teaching assistant'.

The term 'tutor' has been favored for this article in accordance with the policy of the English Department at the Philipps University Marburg. The decision was additionally supported by strong similarities to the German use of this term. Here, tutors are undergraduates as well as graduate students. The following part will give details about their tasks and fields of application.

4.1 Utilizing tutors in the ICMM

The ICMM as evaluated by Handke (2014, in this volume) is implemented in seminars and practice oriented courses (German: Übung). Therefore, the structure and applied teaching methods of the in-class phase differ considerably from the format of lectures. The following will give a brief overview of the teaching concept used at the Linguistic Department of the Philipps University Marburg.

According to Handke (2013), the course instructor in an *Inverted Classroom Mastery Model* scenario can take advantage of the results of the integrated formative assessment and, in the in-class meeting, assign different exercises to individual groups of students. These groups could then be given special attention by the course instructor since less time[1] is spent with the presentation of new content (cf. Handke, 2013: 19). Depending on the mastery level, the focus during the in-class session will be on repetition and explanation or on practice and discussion (cf. Handke, 2013). A detailed evaluation of the model is given by Handke in this volume (Handke, 2014: 15ff.).

Focusing on and supporting these groups of students is, however, a great challenge in seminars and practice-oriented courses with more than 70 students with only the course instructor being present[2]. The classroom settings such as equipment, seating etc. may pose additional obstacles. Thus, practicing and deepening of content as well as the transfer of new concepts face multiple challenges in larger ICM auditoriums (cf. Günther, 2013; Spannagel C. / Spannagel J., 2013).

With a distinctively higher number of first semester students in the winter term 2013/2014, the course 'Introduction to Linguistics', which had already been taught based in the ICM in the past with a number of about 40 students, now consisted of almost 300 students[3]. The course 'Phonetics, Phonology and Transcription' was split into two groups, i.e. A and B. Group A consisted of both teaching degee and bachelor students, group B was only attended by teaching degree students. On average, the class was attended by about 120 students. With such a great number individual supervision and guidance can hardly be implemented without additional support.

Hence, in the winter term 2013/2014 five student tutors were utilized for the first time in the ICMM in the courses 'Introduction to Linguistics' and 'Phonetics, Phonology and Transcription'. Usually, two to three tutors were alternately assigned to sessions of either classes, covering all three class dates (cf. Floyd et al., 2014: 40). One important goal was

---

1 In the case of the linguistic classes at Marburg University, hardly any time is consumed by the presentation of new content.

2 Methods which can be used in large lectures in combination with the Inverted Classroom Model are described by Spannagel C. / Spannagel J. (2013: 144 ff.).

3 252 teaching degree students and 44 students in the Bachelor program were enrolled at the beginning of the term, 245 resp. 43 had finally registered for the class via the campus management system. Due to shortages of personnel, the originally four groups were merged into one group for the class 'Introduction to Linguistics' for both, teaching degree and bachelor students.

to support the instructor during the in-class sessions and, thus, ensuring a practice and learner-orientated teaching scenario. All tutors were employed based on a 20 hour per month contract as student assistants over a period of 5 months.

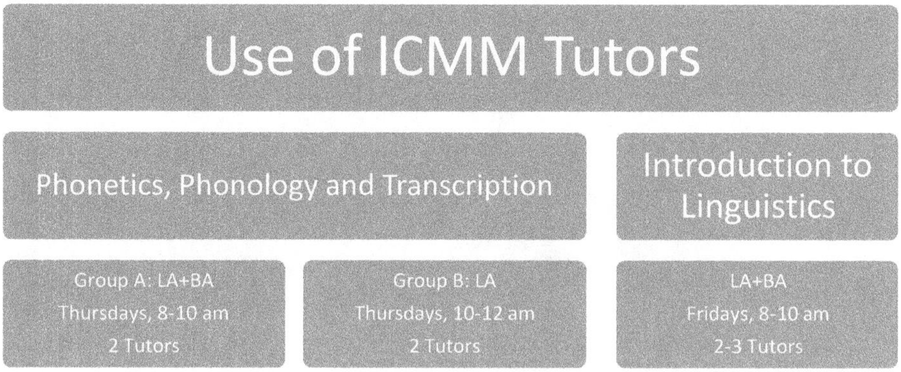

Figure 4.1: Diagram visualizing the use of tutors in different linguistics classes

The selected tutors assumed a special function and were assigned a variety of different tasks. Tasks, challenges and resulting problems will be dealt with in detail in the following chapter.

4.2 Tasks, problems and resulting requirements

ICMM tutors at the English Department were confronted with a variety of different tasks – prior to, during and after classes. These tasks were accompanied by different problems which require a wide range of qualities by the tutors. Those aspects are described in the following chapter.

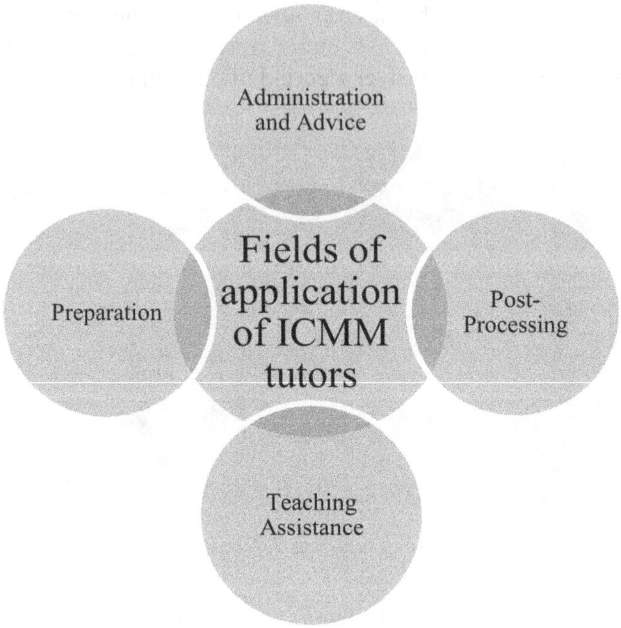

Figure 4.2: Overview of the different fields of application the tasks derive from.

In general, the tutors supported the lecturer in order to ensure an active, student-centered in-class phase focusing on the application and the transfer of new content. With numbers exceeding 300 enrolled first semester students in both, the teaching and the bachelor degree, the tutors were also given administrative tasks throughout the whole semester.

4.2.1 Administrative and counseling tasks

As all first semester students needed to register for the respective classes on the *Virtual Linguistics Campus*[4], one of the very first tasks was concerned with informing the new students about the registration process during the orientation week. For this purpose, tutors prepared a concise handout and gave a short presentation during the general information event explaining the different steps of the registration.

After having registered for the respective *Virtual Linguistics Campus* classes, access had to be granted, passwords reset, and changes of slots arranged (cf. Floyd et al., 2014: 41). Since there were three different time slots for the two courses (see Figure 4.1), it had to be made sure that all students were assigned to the right group, e.g. the group designated for their degree program or that matching the students' timetable the best.

The tutors used different ways to forward information and to assist the students. General information on room or time changes, the content to be prepared, assignments and their

[4] The *Virtual Linguistics Classroom* is the world's largest e-education platform for linguistic content.

corresponding deadlines as well as the final exam was passed along via email[5], in a closed *Facebook*[6] group, and during weekly office hours (cf. Floyd et al, 2014: 42). During the office hours, the tutors answered questions on online model solutions for the latest (graded) worksheets and practical exercises. Additionally, they assisted during the final exams by supervising the students. In cases where students had very little accesses to the online content and/or no worksheet submissions prior to the in-class meetings, they offered help directly via email to the students and reminded them of the necessity of thorough preparation.

The use of the closed *Facebook* group did not only serve as a means to spread information quickly but also as a peer discussion group. With 182 members the community was able to answer a variety of content-related questions themselves and solved problems with very little interference by the tutors. Since all questions and answers were accessible to every group member, the *Facebook* group served as a forum as well as a source for reference (cf. Floyd et al., 2014, Chapter 4.4 in this volume).

4.2.1.1 Problems & resulting requirements

Using modern information and communication technology to such a great extent and the increased use of social media were accompanied by certain problems. Certain skills can be derived from those problems as essential or supplementary for student tutors in ICMM classrooms.

Problem 1: Students expected the tutors to answer questions or to clarify problems within a short period of time. Especially, the use of *Facebook*[7] as a means to spread information put the tutors in a position where demanding requests via email or personal Facebook messages exceeded their working hours as the requests reached into their personal lives.

An important skill in this context is the ability to consciously control the amount of time spent on a particular task, e.g. answering questions via email or on Facebook, and to adhere to the overall limit of working hours based on one's contract. Apart from the time, or better, self management, the tutors need to be aware of the responsibilities and limitations of their work and accept the fact that certain problems cannot be solved immediately or that it may not even be their responsibility to solve them.

---

5 A special staff email address was used for the communication between the students and the tutors throughout the semester.

6 The course instructor for the class was no member of this group and had no access to what had been communicated in this group between the students and tutors.

7 Although the tutors had planned for the students to use the closed Facebook group to discuss content-related question without any interference, in the course of the semester the students' expectations rose and the number and intensity of requests for further comments and clarification increased.

Communicating in a polite but confident way is constantly required and the tutors must be reassured that referring to office hours or to the possibility of self study is an appropriate way of dealing with some of the students' requests.

Box 4.1: Communicative and self-competence as requirements in context of social media

Problem 2: In those cases where the communication between the course instructor and the tutors was not optimized / aligned, incorrect information caused confusions that the tutors had to clarify later on.

This is certainly not an ICMM specific problem. Thus, communicative competences are an essential requirement for tutors in both a traditional and ICMM setting. Moreover, target-oriented behavior and organizational skills *foster the communication process.*

Box. 4.2: Organizational skills as important factors of successful administration

Problem 3: The tutors were presented with criticism and frustration on multiple levels and in different itensities. They needed to decide which to pass on to the course instructor in order to foster the student's learning process.

A very basic but essential skill in this context is the ability to accept criticism and to act professionally. Since the reasons for criticism are diverse, an important skill is the ability to filter the information and to reflect on its sources. Therefore, tutors need to be able to reflect critically on the in-class meetings and on their own actions during and after class.
Moreover, an important quality concerns the ability to work in a team. The tutors highly benefit from mutual support and cooperation.

Box. 4.3: The ability to acknowledge criticism and to work in a team as essential qualities of ICMM tutors

The tasks can further be differentiated into those concerning the preparation, the in-class activities, and the post-processing.

4.2.2 Tasks prior to the in-class meetings: Preparation

Tutors in ICCM-based teaching settings face administrative and content-related tasks. They took turns in preparing different kinds of material and attended regular meetings with the course instructor.

In every in-class session, a number of content-related questions were asked to elicit the degree of preparation by the students for this particular session. For this purpose, an audience response system was used. One of the tutors' tasks in this context was the technical implementation of the introductory questions with the *ActivInspire* software after the weekly meeting with the course instructor (cf. Floyd et al., 2014: 40). Since the instructor made use of the *ActiVote* devices, the tutors were also expected to bring the requested number of devices to class and to collect them at the end of the session.

A further task prior to the in-class meetings was the preparation of activities in which students could apply their acquired knowledge in-class. The course instructor arranged weekly meetings with all tutors in order to prepare the aforementioned questions and the activities for the upcoming in-class session as well as to discuss students' feedback. Those meetings were part of their weekly work routine.

More of a private concern for the tutors was the individual preparation of the content ensuring their ability to answer upcoming questions in-class and to anticipate possible problems of students. Tutors were granted access to model solutions and additional material to revise and prepare the content.

4.2.2.1 Problems & resulting requirements

New, additional exercises to apply and transfer knowledge were developed throughout the whole semester as part of the tutors' tasks prior to and after the in-class meetings for both the bachelor and teaching degree students. The tutors worked in teams in order to prepare new material such as worksheet questions and practical exercises as well as the respective solutions. The material was either provided online in the corresponding content unit or handed out as additional exercises during class.

Problem 4: A problem which presented itself primarily during the in-class sessions was the tutors little experience in developing teaching material. Due to their lack of didactical and methodological skills, some misunderstandings, which needed further clarification and explanation, occurred. Especially at the beginning, the exercises were sometimes not matching the degree of difficulty needed for the respective group of learners. Additionally, the number of exercises was either too high or too low.

> *An important feature in this context is the ability to structure the additional exercise material (the learning process), develop teaching aims and use appropriate methods. Thus, methodological competence and experience in the context of teaching are important qualities ICMM tutors need to develop.*

Box 4.4: Structuring the practical and multimedial exercise material as well as its application in class as important requirements

As mentioned earlier on, the use of modern technology drew upon a certain level of media literacy by the tutors and required them to be able to solve upcoming problems and to fix further technical errors.

Problem 5: Technical devices such as interactive whiteboards, microphones or the audience response system *ActiVote* sometimes caused unexpected difficulties. Technical errors occurred in-class and needed to be fixed instantly. A difficulty in this context was that not every tutor exhibited the same level of competence in handling the equipment and corresponding software.

As a consequence, the tutors need to have great knowledge in using the respective software *and technical devices. Media competence and media literacy is a mandatory requirement of ICMM tutors.*

Box 4.5: Media competence as an essential requirement of ICMM tutors

4.2.3 Tasks during the in-class sessions

An essential task of the student tutors was the assistance during the in-class meetings. Helping students with their practicals[8], checking results and answering questions, and by this, assisting the course instructor in creating an active in-class session, was of major importance for the tutors.

A particular challenge was the fact that both, bachelor and teaching degree students, were taught during the same in-class meeting (cf. Floyd et al, 2014: 42). Since they used different online material, this requested that during the in-class sessions adapted exercises for practicing were provided.

Tutors were also responsible for handing out and collecting the devices used for the poll. They checked the hardware and marked those devices that did not work properly.

One further task was the development of lecture games such as *Taboo* and its implementation in-class (cf. Spannagel C. / Spannagel J., 2013: 117f.).

4.2.3.1 Problems & resulting requirements

Since the students used both, videos and online material, to prepare for the in-class sessions, they acquired a deep knowledge of the different fields within the discipline of linguistics. As a result, the questions asked were much more detailed and exceeded the content of the corresponding online session.

Problem 6: As some questions were particularly detailed or concerned topics from following sessions, the tutors could not always answer those questions right away or felt insecure with their given answer.

A necessary criterion for each tutor in the ICM, as in traditional teaching scenarios, is a high level of subject competence. Although the presence of the course instructor in class is a major advantage compared to the traditional tutoring scenarios, checking answers with the instructor is not always possible. Thus, the tutors not only need to prepare themselves thoroughly but also have to be able to anticipate questions and possible obstacles in the different fields of linguistics.

Box 4.6: Subject competence as an important aspect within this tutoring concept

[8] A practical is a set of tasks to be solved in-class which aim at the transfer of the newly acquired content. Practicals are part of the online units (cf. Handke, 2014: 17).

Problem 7: A further challenge, apart from high student numbers, was the fact that students from both the teaching degree and the bachelor degree were taught together. Besides additional exercises that had to be prepared, the in-class session had to be adapted to the needs of both groups – the teaching degree and the bachelor students.

This demanded that the tutors are able to organize the group of about 40 bachelor students in the same lecture hall and to assist them during the phase of practicing and knowledge transfer. Besides organizational skills, an outgoing personality and leadership qualities add to the requirements of ICMM tutors.
Moreover, the tutors have to have a high level of competence within the particular subject area in order to assist the students of both degrees. Since the tutors also check the results, they are expected to be able to revise and explain concepts and to adapt to different learning levels.

Box 4.7: Aspects of personality and experience with different study programs and groups of learners as supplementary requirements for ICMM tutors

4.2.4 Tasks following the in-class meetings: Post-processing

Quality assurance of primarily the online content, the respective practicals and worksheets is one important task succeeding the in-class meetings. Through regular revision of online material, the post-processing constitutes a major aspect of quality assurance together with the preparatory tasks.

Based on the feedback of the students and on own observations, the tutors corrected mistakes and improved the quality of exercises and further online content. They also developed completely new tasks and increased the pool of task types available for formative assessment.

4.2.4.1 Problems and resulting requirements

The problems and required skills and competences are similar to those of the tasks prior to the in-class meetings. The development of the new and the revision of existing material are mutually important tasks of both phases; the problems are quite similar and need not to be mentioned again. For a description of related problems and necessary skills, consult section 4.2.2.1.

Figure 4.3 summarizes the required qualities by the tutors in the different fields of application. The requirements are not exclusive but rather those most important for the respective tasks. Methods of assessing those requirements are described in section 4.3.

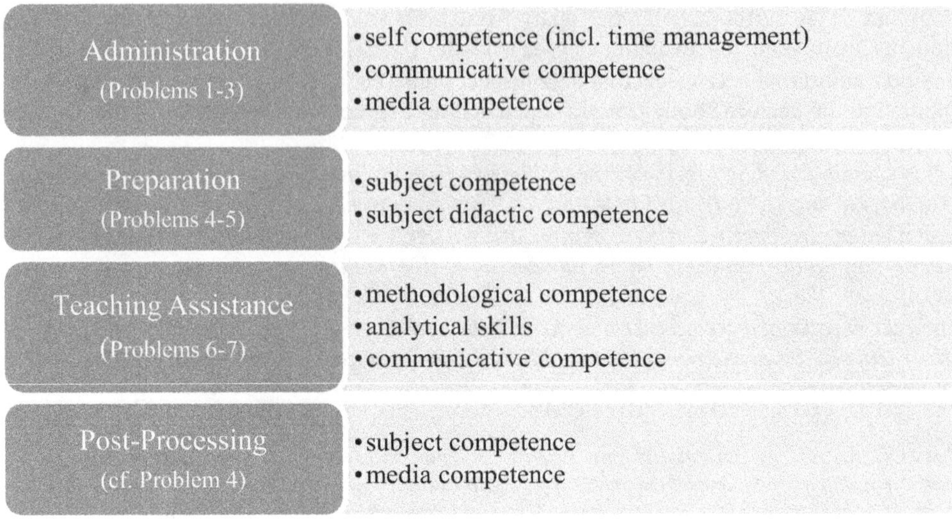

Figure 4.3: Overview of the requirements deriving form the four fields of applications and the observed problems.

4.3 Selection process and assessment methods

As this specific form of tutoring as described here demands characteristics different from those needed for the traditional tutoring model, new ways of assessing the suitability of an applicant are called for. Additionally, due to the fact that this is a novel model, no selection process or assessment methods have been established yet.

First and foremost, one needs to ensure the applicants fulfill the necessary and only jointly sufficient characteristics needed for this tutoring model. Testing for and ensuring the desired requirements proofed to be a challenge, especially when it came to soft skills. From the above description of the fields of application for the tutors (administration, preparation, teaching assistance & post-processing), the following required competences and skills have been identified for the selection process (see Figure 4.4):

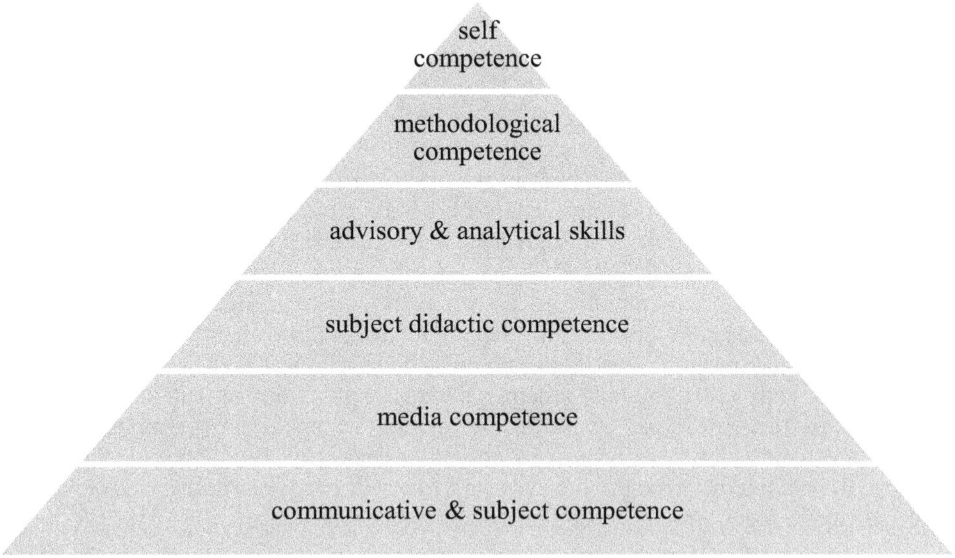

Figure 4.4: Pyramid of required skills and competence for successful ICM tutoring

To ensure the necessary level of subject specific knowledge and proficiency (subject competence), the traditional way of referring to the applicants' transcripts of records[9] [cf. INT1& INT2] is of course used for the ICMM tutor selection process as well. However, recent experience has shown that this might not be a sufficient enough tool as a deeper, more wholesome knowledge is required from the tutors to answer the students' questions which have proven to go quite frequently far beyond the session or course content. A vast range of linguistic knowledge, therefore, needs to be readily available. Having the prospective tutors take actively part in one session might serve well in establishing their abilities to handle transfer questions and situations in which they are out of their depth. Furthermore, their ability to quickly adapt to new situations (next group – new set of questions, different background knowledge, diverse types of learners etc.) can be judged through their performance in class (subject didactic compentence/ analytical skills/ methodological competence).

Prospective tutors need to be able to interact, deal with and handle individuals as well as groups. An outgoing personality is quite advantageous here. The in-class situation will also show whether they work well or are able to concentrate even when exposed to a constant noise level such as will present itself during the sessions (cf. Floyd et al, 2014: 44). In addition, their interactions with the students will give some indication as to their abilities to explain issues adequately, so their teaching skills may be tested with this method (subject didactic competence).

Additionally, their performance in class as students themselves might give insights into their capabilities in the respective subject. Further, their in-class behavior may also give indications about otherwise difficult to judge characteristics such as reliability. Here the

9 Here, the grade points in the linguistics and language practice modules are most interesting.

knowledge of instructors can be utilized in form of referrals. Using referrals or recommendations to ensure the quality of tutoring is a well-established method at American universities and colleges [cf. INT 1; INT 2].

Moreover, a questionnaire designed specifically to test for a broader knowledge base could be used. By adding further not content-related questions, such a questionnaire could also be used to evaluate behavior in specific situations as a first means to establish the level of soft skills. Role-playing scenarios are here of use as well. They are used quite frequently in the academic field in English speaking countries to test or train prospective tutors [cf. INT 1; INT 3; INT 4; INT 5]. Specific, often high stress and/or standard situations (i.e. conflict situations, debates, email correspondences or confronting applicants with questions exceeding their knowledge) are helpful to review the prospective tutors' reaction and their suitability for their future tasks (communicative competence). This will also show whether the applicants work well under pressure or when put on the spot. How they handle written or spoken correspondences will demonstrate their abilities in respect to politeness aspects. Other aspects, such as the ability to draw a line between private and work life, will only present themselves through time and cannot factor into the selection process (self-competence).

As the ICMM makes highly use of modern teaching technologies (interactive whiteboards, audience response systems, tablet-PCs, e-learning platforms etc.), prospective tutors need to be able to use such devices. Therefore, their media literacy needs to be appraised as well. This can be done by having the applicants prepare and use exercises in class, e.g. '*ActiVote* questions' or HTML 5 based multimedia content and exercises, along with having them write practicals and solutions for the e-education platform (analytical skills). The ability to create exercises for the e-education platform and for use in-class is highly valued in this tutoring model as quality assurance plays a major role especially when striving to improve the content used on- and offline. The tutors are integrally involved in this process and need to be able to contribute appropriately in accordance to in-class experience (ability to self-reflect).

4.4 Quality assurance

Maintaining and improving quality is one of the most important issues for the future. Refining the selection process is one measure employed to this end. Peer training is another important pillar of quality assurance as well as constant feedback from the students and the acting tutors. Feedback helps to reflect on how well tasks and methods used in class have functioned and which changes and/or adjustments need to be made for future runs.

Peer training has previously been impossible as no tutors had ever worked within this new framework. Now that first experiences have been made, the following generations of tutors will be able to draw from the newly acquired know-how of those pioneer ICMM-tutors. By reviewing past performances via peer discussions, student feedback and the insights of the instructor, it becomes possible to draw conclusions and implement improvements, as well as make adjustments after problems are identified and suitable solutions are found.

However the question maintains: What needs to or can be done to increase quality even more? How can the necessary skills of individual tutors be improved? How can the quality of the model be maintained or even increased?

Possible answers were found in following measures:

For one, the Hochschuldidaktik Marburg intern (HD-M^{IN}) offers a special workshop for trainers of tutors which concludes in a certificate. This workshop is called 'Train-the-Tutor' (TTT) and conveys information on how to teach basic didactic aspects of tutoring and self-competence to prospective or active tutors. So not only didactic aspects are a focus, but also responsibilities and limitations of tutors are pointed out to the coaches as they need to make the future tutors aware of and help them to identify their role as tutors. The so trained coaches can then help prospective and active tutors to lay a didactic base for their upcoming tasks. They function therefore as multiplier and help ensure the quality of future tutors.

Furthermore, apart from the foundation course, the HD-M^{IN}'s tutor training program (TUQ) offers different workshops such as 'presentation and visualization', 'communication – in difficult situations' and 'methods – working with groups' [INT6]. The tutors can partake in workshops just to improve their didactic or media skills besides other competences or they may decide to do a specified amount of courses concluding their efforts with a certificate which is additionally useful for future careers.

Right now, the authors are developing a specialization module for the ICMM within this program with the following foci:

- Preparation for working with large groups
- Developing / deepening media compentce
- Familiarize tutors with the ICMM
- Practising in-class situations (role-play / simulations, confront with possible difficulties ➔ raise awareness, develop awareness of problems)
- Develop self-competence / soft skills (private status as student vs. work relationship with fellow students)

This specialization module will first be offered October 2014 before lectures start in the winter term.

Additionally, SMART Board trainings are offered by our research group and the university to familiarize students with the interactive whiteboards (IWBs) which are installed in all seminar rooms of the English Department. The tutors can use those training sessions to improve their media literacy and prepare for their future tasks in which the IWBs will play an important part.

The constant refinement of the selection process as well as the use of experienced tutors to train newly incoming ones additionally helps to assure quality of the ICMM tutoring program.

4.5 Conclusion and outlook

The use of student tutors is a fairly new development within the ICMM. This tutoring concept where students are *"on par with the class instructor"* (Handke, 2014: 31) has been implemented for the first time in the winter term 2013/2014. It offers the possibility of increasing learner-centeredness and the implementation of a problem-based teaching approach within larger ICM-based classes. The regular presence of the postgraduate student tutors in class supports the course instructor so active group work phases and lively discussions on new concepts can be assured.

This article shows that tutors in the ICMM have to face multiple tasks and challenges inside and outside the classroom. Besides assisting the course instructor during the in-class meetings, their tasks evolve around administration, counseling and preparation of online material. A part of the concept is the development of new exercise material to be used in class for the group activities. This accounts for a part of their follow-up tasks during the post-procession of single sessions and the class as a whole.

Different problems have been observed which can be reduced through thorough preparation, i.e. the careful selection and subsequent coaching of new tutors. As the tutors need a great variety of different skills, this variety has to be reflected in the selection process as well. Therefore, special tools of assessment are needed to ensure the necessary requirements are met by prospective tutors.

As tutor trainers, the authors are excited to see the progress of the tutoring induced by the new specialization in the tutor training designed especially for the ICMM tutoring model. During the subsequent semester, different aspects such as the proposed methods of tutor selection, the fields of application of tutors, their problems and success as well as the training concept will be further evaluated.

4.6 References

Floyd, Jennifer et al. 2014. Student Tutors in ICMM Courses in Academic Teaching: First Experiences. In this volume. 27–35.

Handke, Jürgen. 2013. Beyond a Simple ICM. In: Handke, Jürgen/Kiesler, Natalie/Wiemeyer, Leonie (eds.). The Inverted Classroom Model. The 2nd German ICM-Conference – Proceedings. München: Oldenbourg Verlag. 15–20.

Handke, Jürgen. 2014. The Inverted Classroom Mastery Model – A Diary Study. In this volume, 3–22.

Spannagel, Christian/Spannagel, Jana. 2013. Designing In-Class Activities in the Inverted Classroom Model. In: Handke, Jürgen/Kiesler, Natalie/Wiemeyer, Leonie (Eds.). The Inverted Classroom Model. The 2nd German ICM-Conference – Proceedings. München: Oldenbourg. 113–121.

[INT 1] Brigham Young University – Idaho: Tutoring Training Material – Orientation and ABC's of Tutoring.

https://courses.byui.edu/AcademicSupport/tutoring-center/tutor_training/Orientation%20and%20ABC%27s.pdf; last accessed on 28/07/2014.

[INT 2] Viterbo University: Academic Resource Center (ARC) – Becoming a Tutor. http://www.viterbo.edu/administration_and_services/academic_resource_center/Becoming_a_Tutor.aspx; last accessed on 28/07/2014.

[INT 3] Viterbo University: Academic Resource Center (ARC) – Tutor Training Manual. http://www.viterbo.edu/uploadedFiles/administration_and_services/academic_resource_center/TutorTrainingManual.pdf

[INT 4] University of Hawaii. Kilohana: The Academic Success Center – New Tutor Training Role Play Scenarios. http://hilo.hawaii.edu/kilohana/documents/TutoringScenarios.pdf; last accessed on 28/07/2014.

[INT 5] Skidmore College – New York: Office of Academic Servides – Tutoring Manual. http://www.skidmore.edu/academic_services/documents/tutor-manual.pdf; last accessed on 28/07/2014.

[INT 6] Hochschuldidaktik Marburg intern (HD-M^{IN}): TUQ – Qualifikationsprogramm für Tutorinnen und Tutoren. http://www.uni-marburg.de/einrichtungen/hochschuldidaktik/hdmin/zielgruppen/studierende/wahlpflicht; last accessed on 28/07/2014.

5 Establishment of Structured Comments and Coherent Dialogues Referring to Educational Videos on YouTube

Kerstin Raudonat, Fabian Wiedenhöfer, Dominik Rudisch, Vicdan Burna, Selma Ulusoy, Nicola Marsden, Dominikus Herzberg

In the *Inverted Classroom Model* (ICM) it is of major importance to provide digitized teaching content – especially in the online phase when learners work on their own (cf. Handke/Sperl, 2012). The use of educational videos such as lecture videos is essential for preparing and following up on the learning contents so that time in class can be used for deepening the subject, exercises, and discussions (cf. Fischer/Spannagel, 2012). Therefore, the necessity to discuss teaching materials and content questions arises outside the classroom. An important aspect in the learning process is comparing notes with other learners and asking lecturers questions. This requires suitable communication options via digital media such as discussion forums and commentary functions which essentially provide learners with the opportunity to comment on provided media and their content. To allow for organizing coherent dialogues about educational videos on *YouTube*, the platform *Studystar* was developed.

5.1 Using educational videos in ICM-based teaching and learning settings

Educational videos are a primary means to deliver teaching material in ICM-based teaching and learning settings. The videos are not only recorded lectures; videos can differ in type and content. Referring to the content, Loviscach (2013) distinguishes primarily between *„expository lectures", "worked examples", "deconstruction of misconceptions", "recordings of tutoring"* and *"video documentations"* (2013: 5f.). Each kind of video focuses on a special form of presenting learning contents – from explaining a theory to documenting a problem solution step by step. Videos can also differ in regards to the design and their interaction mode: from a one-to-one recording of a lecture to creating videos with edited screens, narration, and legends. Lecturers have many possibilities to present learning content in videos for students. The question which arises is how learners evaluate these videos and how they use them.

Largent (2013) explicates the following evaluative questionnaire's findings in an experience report about courses using lecture videos: More than half of the course participants agreed that the offered lecture videos were beneficial to their ability to learn. Around half stated that they wished other tutors would use lecture videos as well (cf. Largent, 2013: 90). A study by Carlisle (2010) revealed similar results, and he concluded that creating videos can be a good way to get students to engage with the material before coming to class. Fischer and Spannagel (2012) stated in their study that the majority of the students watched the lecture videos before coming to class. Most of them watched a video once and in doing so repeated specific parts when necessary. Only a small minority used the video again to repeat and follow up on the learning content after class. A majority of the students reported that they learn more easily with lecture videos than in traditional lectures (cf. Fischer/Spannagel, 2012: 232). But these findings do not reveal anything about the quality of the learned contents regarding correctness.

Loviscach (2013) explicitly names the problem of misconceptions and proposes the use of special videos which address known misunderstandings and deconstruct them (2013: 6). A proper way to try to minimize problems related to understanding content would also be to discuss them immediately as they arise. In this case, students and lecturers need to have suitable digital communication options. It is important that these options are created in a way that allows and supports coherent dialogues.

5.2 Coherence and multiple threading in computer mediated communication

Establishing conversational coherence is an important part of communication. It refers to the extent of communicators responding to each other and the ability to establish and maintain common issues (cf. Cornelius, 2001). Ensuring coherence in computer mediated communication, particularly in asynchronous settings, is more challenging than in face-to-face communication (cf. Schweizer, 2006). To keep the thread through a conversation in asynchronous media it has to be clear to which statement a comment refers, especially in long comment tracks. It is even more important to establish coherence in case of multiple threading. If a conversation, for example in a chat or in a forum, splits up in different issues, it is difficult to identify which statements belong to each theme – the more participants and statements there are, the more complex it becomes. To understand the line of communication, users need to structure comments. It would be convenient to have a technical option that supports structuring. Especially for the discussion of videos, it is vital that it is easy to find out and recognize to which point in time or to which part of the video a comment refers to. Video platforms such as *YouTube* offer means to add comments, but they lack advanced features beyond listing a linear sequence of comments and indenting replies.

5.3 Discussing educational videos on *YouTube* – needs and problems

Many lecturers use *YouTube* for the distribution of educational videos to their students. On this platform, comments are listed one below the other in the order of their appearance. For this reason, the structure of dialogues and relations between single comments are hardly comprehensible for the users – the more comments the more confusing. The process of organizing coherent dialogues is strongly impaired and sometimes even impossible. There is a need for a function which allows the users to attach comments to other ones and structure dialogues with regard to the content in that way.

A reference to a specific point in time in the video can only be accomplished with a textual, structured time declaration – a so-called 'deeplink' – in the comment text. Finding comments on a specific part of the video, for instance questions or additional explanations, is a laborious and time-consuming exercise. An example:

A student watches a video lecture and is confused about an explanation given by the lecturer. A spontaneous reaction is to look for other comments and check whether someone else has had the same problem in understanding and, more interestingly, if someone else has contributed some valuable information for clarifying matters. Currently, the student has to browse through all posted comments. A linear search is neither effective nor user friendly. Evidently, the student needs a feature that pins comments on a timeline with regards to the points in time of the video – both for reading and for posting comments. Such a feature provides a contextual setting for postings that belong and refer to the same part of the video and is a prerequisite to organize comments in coherent dialogues.

We addressed the lack of coherent dialogues in *YouTube* by developing an 'add-on' that mimics the appearance of the *YouTube* website but provides extensive features for comments.

5.4 The platform *Studystar*: features and functioning

Studystar was developed by students of Heilbronn University[1], it uses the *YouTube* functions and has a similar design to *YouTube*. The platform *Studystar* can be reached by the following URL:

http://studystar.se.hs-heilbronn.de

Studystar is a website which dynamically embeds *YouTube* videos and adds functions which *YouTube* does not offer. These functions enable users to structure comments and to arrange them on the video timeline. Users uploading a video can also easily create subdivisions into chapters which are shown as previews in the sidebar. Figure 5.1 shows the user interface:

Figure 5.1: User interface of Studystar

[1] Students of the Heilbronn University developed this platform as part of the 'Lab for Software Projects' in the 4th semester of the Bachelor study programme Software Engineering. The sourcecode is opensource, licenced under the GNU GENERAL PUBLIC LICENSE Version 3 and available on GitHub: https://github.com/F1ll3r/studystar

The right sidebar contains the chapter overview with previews and time codes for each chapter. The additional timeline for comments is below the video and shows the positions of the comments already in existence. The comments in the timeline are shown beneath and appear by mouse-over or click on the timeline position.

The most important feature is the linking of comments to the additional timeline so that users can create comments according to their temporal location in the video[2]. Accordingly, existing comments are shown in the timeline and are indicated at the corresponding point in time while playing the video. Another significant feature is the option to attach comments to other comments. With these two features, follow-up communication is possible: comments are shown at the exact point they were inserted and other users can again comment on them. This enables coherent dialogues which refer to a concrete video scene.

In addition, users can create private comments that other users cannot see. This way, students can work on an educational video and directly note questions, remarks, or any thoughts of interest. These notations are helpful in the learning process and useful for handling the video later.

The mechanism behind *Studystar* analyses comments and puts them in a time context instead of just listing and sorting comments like *YouTube* does. *Studystar* does not use its own database. Instead, the API (Application Programming Interface) of the *YouTube* commenting system to read and store comments is instrumented, a time stamp is encoded in the text field of a comment. Comments which are natively posted on *YouTube* and contain a time code are also shown in the additional timeline below the video. Multiple queries using jQuery and the *YouTube* Data API are necessary to collect all comments of a video. Regular expressions are used to distinguish comments without time information from the ones with time information; the latter are attached and located in the timeline below the video.

An overview of the chapters of a video helps users easily navigate through a video. *Studystar* uses the video description and regular expressions to produce a visual overview with a picture taken from the video. Figure 5.2 contrasts the displays of chapter overviews on *YouTube* and *Studystar*:

[2] For this users need a google account and respectively have to login.

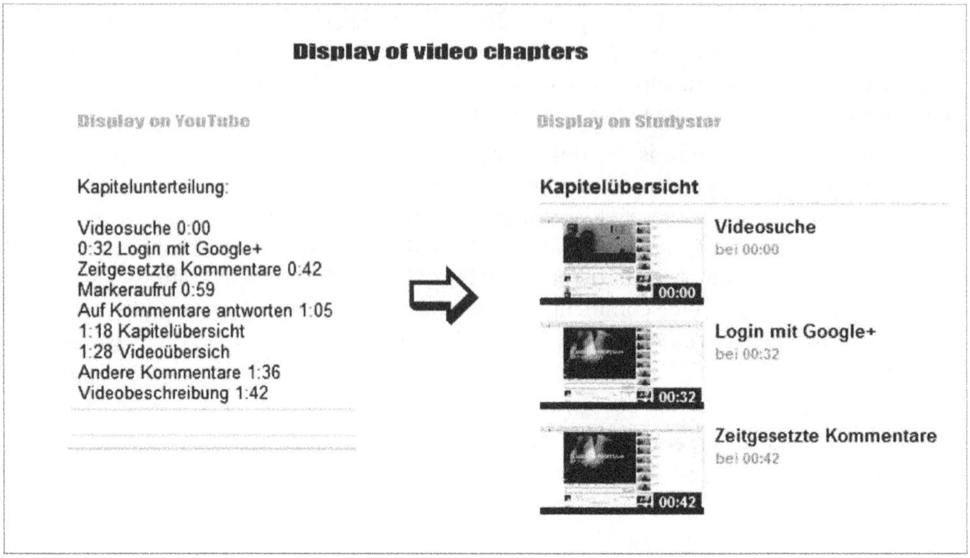

Figure 5.2: Display of video chapters on YouTube *and* Studystar

YouTube shows the description of the chapter names and the corresponding time codes. *Studystar* creates a pictorial chapter overview. The single chapters are visualised in the timeline as well. It is not possible to get a preview of scenes given an arbitrary time stamp due to a current limitation of the *YouTube* API. The API provides only three preview pictures: one picture of the beginning, one of the middle, and one of the end of the video.

Studystar dynamically embeds *YouTube* videos based on the given video ID by *YouTube* and uses the same Path ("/watch") and Query String ("?v=VIDEOID"). This can be illustrated by an example:

YouTube URL: https://www.youtube.com/watch?v=O-BTYodGrdM
Studystar URL: http://studystar.se.hs-heilbronn.de/watch?v=O-BTYodGrdM

Using this technique *Studystar* can be easily used with any available video on *YouTube*.

5.5 Conclusion

In the context of the ICM, the presented functions of *Studystar* enable users to handle educational videos in the learning processes in an effective and dialogue-oriented way. Learners can directly take individual notes in the video timeline and ask questions to particular video contents. They can share their questions and discuss them with other learners in coherent comment tracks. The comment system of *Studystar* is also beneficial for lecturers; they receive time-related and thereby content-related feedback on their teaching materials, which they can use as the basis for improvements in their videos.

They can participate in the dialogue, clear up misunderstandings, and provide additional information if required.

For the future, extensions are considered which allow filtering and comment ratings so that users can even more easily identify relevant comments on a video. Further improvements shall be developed and implemented based on the feedback of users.

5.6 References

Carlisle, Martin C. 2010. Using YouTube to Enhance Student Class Preparation in an Introductory Java Course. Proceedings of SIGCSE '10. New York: ACM. 470–474.

Cornelius, Caroline 2001. Gegenseitiges Verständnis in Computerkonferenzen: Voraussetzungen und Folgen konversationaler Kohärenz in Entscheidungsfindungsgruppen im Medienvergleich. Berlin: Waxmann.

Fischer, Maike/Spannagel, Christian. 2012. Lernen mit Vorlesungsvideos in der umgedrehten Mathematikvorlesung. In: Desel, Joerg/Haake, Joerg M./Spannagel, Christian (eds.), DeLFI 2012 - Die 10. e-Learning Fachtagung Informatik der Gesellschaft für Informatik e.V.. Bonn: Köllen. 225–236.

Handke, Jürgen/Sperl, Alexander (eds.). 2012. Das Inverted Classroom Model. Begleitband zur ersten deutschen ICM-Konferenz. München: Oldenbourg.

Largent, David 2013. Flipping a large CSO course: An experience report about exploring the use of video, clickers and active learning. Journal of Computing Sciences in Colleges, 29 (1), 84–91.

Loviscach, Jörn. 2013. The Inverted Classroom: Where to Go from Here. In: Handke, Jürgen/ Kiesler, Natalie/Wiemeyer, Leonie (eds.). 2013. The Inverted Classroom Model. The 2nd German ICM-Conference – Proceedings. München: Oldenbourg. 3–14.

Schweizer, Karin. 2006. Moderation und Steuerung der netzbasierten Wissenskommunikation. Frankfurt a. M.: Peter Lang.

III Implementations of the ICM at University Level

In recent years, the *Inverted Classroom Model* (ICM) has been implemented at higher education institutions across Germany and world-wide. The ICM conference held in Marburg in 2012 was a starting point towards ICM-based teaching. In the meantime, a shift away from mere content production towards an expansion and individual adjustments of the model has taken place. The latest ICM conference provided a forum for the exchange of ideas and methods as well as first-hand experience reports.

Volkmar Langer, Knut Linke and Florian Schimanke have investigated how ICM-based teaching and learning support students during their learning activities. They have been using the ICM in Business Computer Science studies at the University of Applied Sciences Hameln. A major goal of their new concept of teaching is the development decision-making competences and the increase of practical orientation in the module 'Computer Networks'.

Combining different e-learning elements for the online phase and the idea of project-based learning has proved to be very beneficial for students of 'Service Learning' at the University of Augsburg. In his experience report, Philip Meyer describes a variant of the ICM with a special adjustment in the practice phase. Group work, face-to-face experience and constant reflection on the learning process play an important role, as discussed by Meyer.

In their article, Oliver Kreutz and his colleagues report on the implementation of the ICM in Law Studies at the University of Göttingen. The project evaluation shows that ICM implementation is a chance to activate students in a university setting and to motivate them to take responsibily for their learning. With the new concept for the course 'Media Law' and the development of new e-learning elements for self-guided learning, they catered for different learner types and allowed for a highly practice-oriented in-class phase.

6 Improvement of Self-directed Learning by Using the *Inverted Classroom Model* (ICM) for a Basic Module in Business Computer Sciences

Volkmar Langer, Knut Linke, Florian Schimanke

How can the teaching and learning method *Inverted Classroom Model* (ICM) support students during their learning activities? How can the time inside the classroom be used more sustainably by teachers and students for their learning activities? Based on these questions, this paper provides examples from the usage of the ICM in the module 'Computer Networks', which serves as a fundamental module in the Business Computer Sciences studies at the HSW-University of Applied Sciences. The ICM was used in this context to develop a new educational concept for the mentioned module, aiming to provide a cooperative learning environment during the time of attendance in class. In our scenario, the lecturers became learning facilitators to a greater extent than the traditional teacher typically does. The main target of this new concept is to increase the practical orientation based on the learners' requirements and to provide them with a higher level of sustainable and well-trained decision-making competence. In this article we describe the concept development, the necessary preparations, and the realization of the ICM integration, including a brief reflection through evaluations of the teaching concept by bachelor students over the course of two years.

6.1 Introduction

The Bologna Process has led to serious changes for the quality assurance of education and the transparency of teaching and learning content. This includes an appropriate determination of the workload for the students in bachelor and master courses. Courses which have a similar aim regarding teaching and learning targets are merged into modules. The examinations in each module cover the material from each of its component courses. However, what has not changed much since the Bologna Process is the way of learning and teaching. Most courses (appr. 89%, comp. Kerres/Schmidt, 2012: 87) are still based on the traditional teaching method of lecturing, courses and tutorials. Self-responsible and self-directed learning, for example through projects, are only used on a sporadic base (2.5% project-based learning methods, comp. Kerres/Schmidt, 2012: 87). Written examinations are still most widely used as proof of performance (67%, comp. Kerres/Schmidt, 2012: 89). This leads to a learning culture that is still focused on examinations and not on students and competence-building. For sustainable learning, it is important to support students in increasing and enhancing their competences and abilities, which leads to better self-organization and decision-making abilities (cf. Erpenbeck, 2007).

In this article it is shown how the *Inverted Classroom Model* (cf. Lage et al., 2000) is used to change a traditional teaching approach in a basic module of an integrated degree program in Business Computer Sciences. After a short introduction to the mentioned model, this article provides information about the former setup of the mentioned module, the new and changed principles of teaching, and a reflection of the experiences during this process.

6.2 Introduction to the *Inverted Classroom Model* (ICM)

In the *Inverted Classroom Model* (or *Flipped Classroom*, Baker, 2000) teaching and learning activities as well as the traditional roles in this context are inverted. This is done with the aim of allowing students to access learning content outside of a lecture by themselves, which provides them with a higher learning individuality based on their individual learning rate, at individual learning places, and at their preferred times. With this approach, the time inside the classroom can be used in a more sophisticated manner, and the in-class actions can be focused on value-added activities. An example for these activities is the *Active Auditorium* (cf. Spannagel C., 2011; Spannagel, C./Spannagel J., 2013), which helps the students to immerse the learning content through discussions and questions and which supports them on their journey to a deeper understanding of it.

The knowledge gained through self-learning can then be transferred to more practical questions through case studies or exercises. This supports the learning process especially when a competence-oriented assessment is used instead of a written examination as proof of performance. If the approach succeeds to provide an added value to in-class activities and to use competence-oriented certifications based on case studies or additional exercises instead of a due date oriented written exam evaluation, the quality in learning should be increased in a sustainable manner (cf. Hattie, 2007).

Simultaneously, the ICM supports the approach of autonomous and non-formal learning. This is highly necessary as Schulmeister and Metzger (2011) have proven in their empirical study of the new Bachelor courses in Germany. In their study, they show that self-learning is not well-integrated in the courses and therefore hardly realized by students. As reason for this, they mention that it is not only the fault of the students and their personal behavior but rather a deficient integration of self-learning parts into the study itself (cf. Schulmeister/Metzger, 2011). With the ICM, the teachers as well as the learners have more opportunities and reasons to use self-learning during a module or a study course.

6.3 'Computer Networks' - A fundamental module in Business Computer Sciences

In our example we are focusing on a fundamental module from our integrated degree program for a Bachelor of Science in Business Computer Sciences. This degree program at the Hochschule Weserbergland is designed as a six semester study and contains the module 'Computer Networks' (Vernetzte IT Systeme) in the third semester. In the official module-description, the aim of the qualification is set as follows: *"The students are familiar with the fundamental terms and concepts of computer networks ... they are able to classify and design local networks by themselves."* [1] The module itself provides fundamentals for further modules like 'Network Management,' 'Network Security' or 'Web Engineering'. As a requirement for the module 'Computer Networks' (CN), students need to successfully pass the module 'Fundamentals of Information Technology' ('Grundlagen der Informatik') in the second semester.

In the past, the CN module was designed as a traditional lecture with additional seminars and practical trainings and was completed with a written exam. In addition, the students had to conduct research on current practices to comply with the requirements of an integrated degree program. This research is done in small groups during the time that students are still working with their companies shortly before the beginning of the semester and is presented during the first lessons of the module in class. The workload of the module is calculated with 5 ECTS credits, which compares to a training time of 150 hours. Those 150 hours are split into the time in class, with 60 hours, and self-learning time, with 90 hours. During the entire time period, our students are assisted and supported site-independently by the respective lecturer through our learning management system (LMS) ILIAS[2]. In our case, the typical size of a student group is 25 students in average.

6.4 A new didactical concept

The primary objective and main goal of the integration of the ICM followed the strategic target to increase the quality and sustainability of learning. With the new didactical concept, not only the distribution of learning content and a shifting of learning time

---

1 Comp. with the module catalogue from the Hochschule Weserbergland for the bachelor degree course 'Bachelor in Business Computer Sciences',http://www.hsw-hameln.de/hsw/wirtschafts informatik---moduluebersicht.phplast accessed on 06/26/2014.

2 Official Webpage of the Open Source Learn-Management-System ILIAS, http://www.ilias.de/ docu, last accessed on 03/24/2014.

should be implemented. It was also tremendously important to enhance in-class time usage and to design the final examination in a more encouraging way [INT 1]. The focus was switched to building sustainable decision making competences instead of learning for a set point in time, such as an examination (cf. Slepcevic-Zach, 2012).

In our new approach to a didactical concept, we designed the learning and teaching scenario as follows. At the beginning of the semester, the students' learning location is still in their companies. They are invited into a virtual course in our LMS and receive their research exercise, which was a group work in the past. This is done to provide the students with initial contact with the topic of computer networks. In the new approach, this setup is changed in a way that the group work was replaced by an individual task. Each student was requested to provide an article for a wiki in the LMS which is related to the topic of the course. For the articles itself, minimum requirements were set, containing a self-made picture, text and additional sources. All content must be produced by the students themselves.

This change is also important for the lecturer of the course as it provides the students with an early opportunity to access knowledge sources in addition to literature. With this approach, the students can choose a practical example for their article. For the information in the respective article, the students then have to investigate and research the topic by themselves. After the wiki article was reviewed and approved by the lecturer, the respective student was granted access to the general course content. Besides standard literature, this content consists of established sets of slides, video learning nuggets, and e-assessments for self-testing. During fall semester 2012/2013, the e-examinations were used to clock the access to the course materials. For each chapter, it was required to receive 80% correct answers on the questionnaires at minimum to get access to the materials of the following chapter. This was changed in fall semester 2013/2014 when the students were allowed to access all content right from the beginning of the semester. In this case the students were required to organize their learning in a more self-directed manner.

In the first group, term 2012/2013, one third of the group had already finished the e-assessments before the first in-class session started. In the second term (2013/2014), when the e-assessments were not required to access the course materials, most students interestingly did not start working on the e-assessments before the end of the semester.

6.4.1 The content preparation process of Video Learning Nuggets

For the content preparation, the module was separated into six chapters, each with varying numbers of sub-chapters. To further support the ICM approach, each sub-chapter of a chapter contains a video learning nugget, which was produced with *Camtasia Studio*[3]. The presentations used in the videos were oriented on best practices and existing suggestions (cf. Loviscach, 2012; Handke, 2013b) and contained established *PowerPoint* teaching materials from the past, which were reproduced to comply with open

[3] Video capture software *Camtasia Studio* by TechSmith, http://www.techsmith.de/camtasia.html, last accessed on 03/24/2014.

educational resources (OER) requirements. During this reproduction, it was also decided to work partly with empty slides and to draw certain models and other content directly into the slides during the presentation. The setting itself was designed as a two-person question and answer scenario, to support an active discussion between the participants.

Figure 6.1: Setting of the video learning nuggets – a two person question and answer scenario.

At the end of the recording sessions, 42 learning nuggets were produced for the course, with durations of 5 to 15 minutes each and mostly slightly less than 10 minutes. The videos were published inside the course on our LMS and as a public playlist on *YouTube*. The *YouTube* playlist received about 4,200 views during the first 8 month of availability. The individual videos reached over 1,600 views each, depending on the respective topic. This is considerably more views than there were students in the different courses.

The production itself was designed as rapid production. This means that small mistakes like a short spelling mistake or harrumph did not lead to a re-recording of a whole video. However, in case that mistakes in form and content occurred during recording, the videos were re-recorded or the mistake was corrected in the post production, for example with an information layer in *YouTube*. During the whole production process, most of the time was spent on creating the slides in order to make them comply with OER requirements and on the post production of the videos. For a 10 minute learning video the actual production time was mostly around 20–25 minutes. The post production time, including the conversion of each video, took around 60–75 minutes for a 10 minute learning video, due to technical limitations of *Camtasia Studio*. Therefore, to create 1 minute of video content, you need to invest at least 2–2.5 minutes, not taking into account the time needed for rendering and content upload. Those aspects are strongly dependent on the available infrastructure and need to be considered as well. In our case, the overall ratio was 10 to 12 minutes production time for 1 minute video content including the additional time needed for rendering and content upload. That time ratio is acceptable for the results, for which mostly positive feedback was provided by the students.

Interestingly, several students even requested to receive downloadable versions of the videos to be more flexible in learning and to view them on mobile devices without needing to use their mobile bandwidth. For those students a *BitTorrent* download was initiated, which helped the OER content to be distributed into that file sharing network.

6.4.2 *Active seminar* – An added value lesson

In-class activities are the most important part of the ICM. Those activities require highly professional preparation since all activities must focus on the respective learners [INT 1]. In our case, we developed a so-called *Active Seminar*, which consists of three phases.

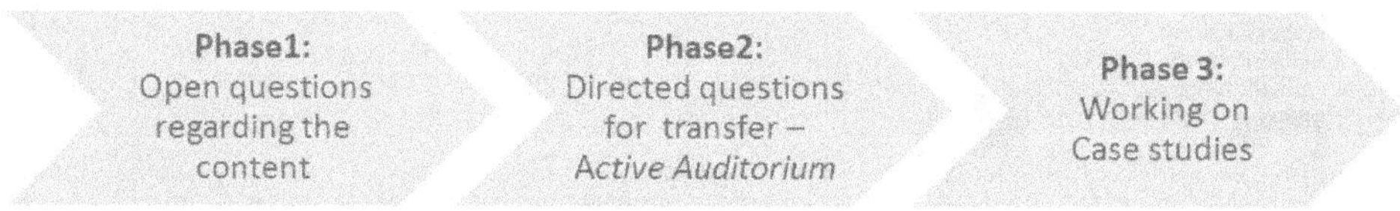

Figure 6.2: The three phases of the Active Seminar

During the first phase, we focused on open questions which were raised by the students about the available learning material and the taught content. In this first phase, which involves a more a classical setting, the lecturer worked out the answers to the questions asked from the auditorium together with the students. In the second phase, the lecturers increased the requirements by providing the students with directed questions. These questions were designed as transfer tasks to support the learners in their ability to transfer theoretical knowledge to the solution of practical problems. This enables the learners to manage their transfer abilities and their current level of theoretical knowledge in combination with their practical knowledge. Those questions were actively discussed in the setting of an *Active Auditorium* (cf. Spannagel C., 2011; Spannagel, C./Spannagel J., 2013), where the lecturers only supported and guided the learners to find a solution for the questions by themselves. Those first two phases were fulfilled in the first half of the course. After that, our third phase started. From this moment the learners were separated into small project groups of 4–5 members. In these small groups, the learners worked on a dedicated and detailed case study on planning a computer network, typically a so-called local area network (LAN), for a small invented company. The approach requires the lecturer to fulfill a dual role. First, he is the virtual contracting authority who requests the network planning, and second, he is the learning guide to support the learners throughout this phase. The result of the case study was a LAN planning paper with approximately 30 pages per group. Those papers were marked as group work. During fall semester 2012/2013, the group work was the sole source for grading. In fall semester 2013/2014, the grading system was changed. Since then, 50% of the grade is fulfilled by the case study and the other 50% is determined through an individual e-assessment via our LMS.

Besides the *Active Seminar*, which replaced the former traditional oriented lecture, a practical tutorial was held. This tutorial allowed the learners to get in practical contact with network components or network applications which may not be available in their respective companies. During fall semester 2012/2013, additional seminars conducted by students of higher semesters were also provided. Those were not continued in 2013/2014 due to lack of student interest.

6.4.3 A change of roles – From lecturer to learning guide

With the implementation of the ICM as a learning and teaching concept, a change of the lecturer's role takes place [INT 1].

This includes a change from traditional knowledge transfer based on the interactionistic model to a learning environment where the lecturer becomes more of a learning guide and learning supporter. In this case, the lecturer becomes responsible for supporting the students in their autonomous learning and self-studies. In the theoretical framework, the term 'facilitation' is recommended for encouragement and support during the learning process [INT 2]. During this process, it should be considered that the new role of a 'facilitator' is more complex than the role of a lecturer during the traditional learning process [INT 2].

In our case and for the used approach of the *Active Seminar* with its three phases in general, the facilitator must fulfill different requirements from different points of view. During the first phase, in which it is necessary to clarify and discuss open questions, students might suffer a lack of an overall impression about the theoretical topic, including the missing of cross-thematic connections.

In this case, it is vital that the lecturer supports the students to make interconnections between the different fields of knowledge in the context of planning a computer network. This also includes minding the students' questions and arranging them in the context of the lecture with its learning goals and targets. During the second phase, the learning supporter should retreat partly and only come into action if students need dedicated support during a practical example in which they seem to lose or miss the educational objective. In this case, the approach of the *Active Auditorium* (cf. Spannagel C., 2011; Spannagel, C./ Spannagel J., 2013) is highly recommendable to provide the students with abilities for checking themselves. In the third phase, the lecturer has to fulfill a dual role. First, he is the virtual contracting authority who requests the LAN planning. As part of this role the lecturer is responsible to provide detailed requirements from a customer's perspective. In this phase the students receive the ability to learn how to interact with customers and which kinds of questions are necessary to understand a customer and his requirements.

The second role, which the lecturer has to fulfill, is the role as learning supporter. This role has the special requirement that the lecturer has to determine how much support a student needs and which part should be done independently by the students. In this phase, the usage of targeted questions and impulses might be helpful to get an insight on the learners' level of knowledge. In addition, each lecturer should take the different group dynamics into consideration and provide support for the different groups accordingly. This can be done, for example, by defining a certain amount of time which the lecturer spends on each group for consultation.

6.5 Reflection and first lessons learned

Preparing for the usage of the ICM was more time-consuming than for the traditional teaching approach. For fall semester 2013/2014, it was decided to produce all video content again in order to modify it according to the feedback from the first year, to rectify mistakes from the first production period and to be able to provide the videos as OER content. The latter made it possible to use *YouTube* as an additional distribution platform now.

The activities from the students in the active seminars were dependent on the time period in the semester. At the beginning of the semester, most questions were related to the available content and regarding a context in which the knowledge must be considered. Due to the lack of linearity, which is normally provided by a traditional class setting, the students need to be supported to implement their questions into such a knowledge network. The amount of the students' questions declined by the end of the first half of the semester but increased again during the final stage of completion of the case study.

In this context, it has to be mentioned that the conversation during the active seminars was marked by professional dialogue, which differs from the experiences with the classical teaching scenario. In addition, students reported a higher perceived workload over the entire semester because they were being challenged more. This statement was confirmed during both fall semesters (2012/2013 and 2013/2014).

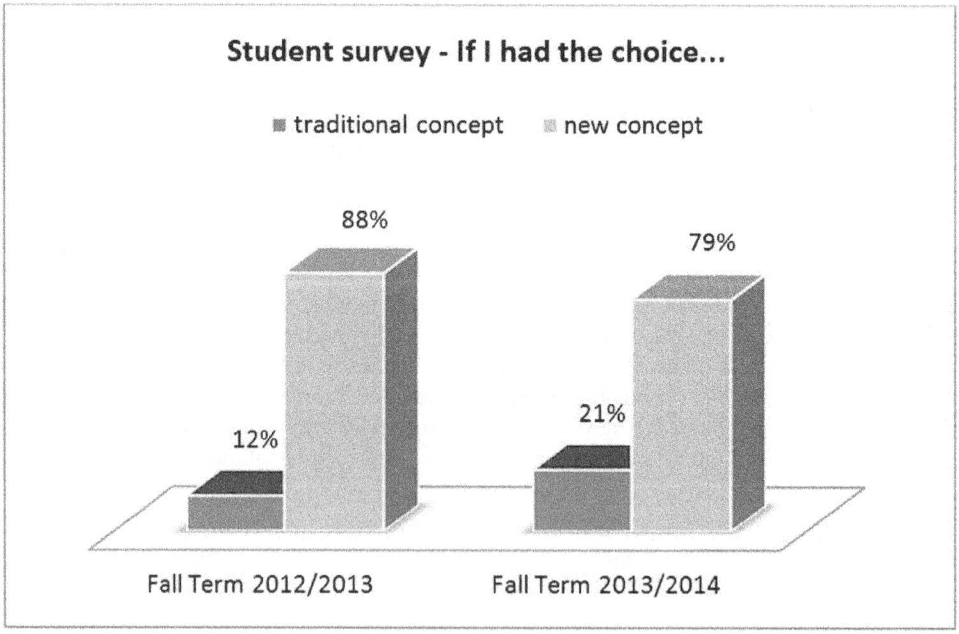

Figure 6.3: Excerpt from the student evaluation.

The final evaluation of the course, which is part of each course at the Hochschule Weserbergland, has shown that the students are satisfied with the new learning approach. 88% of the students of fall semester 2012/2013 and 79% of the students of fall semester 2013/2014 prefer the new (ICM) concept over the traditional approach.[4]

The major challenge for the students during the usage of the ICM in 2012/2013 was the case study. Although half of the time of the *Active Seminar* was allocated for this last phase, not all students were able to transfer their theoretical knowledge successfully to the case study. For fall semester 2013/2014, it was decided to support the students with more dedication. Hence the authors infer that a need for action exists for a closer definition of the guidance and for a more efficient description to transfer theoretical concepts to practical application. In this case, new video nuggets might provide a better and more efficient support. These videos should include real-world footage regarding building installation and electronics to support an earlier transfer of knowledge to practical situations.

From the teaching perspective, the discussions between students and lecturers in both years were more intensive than with the traditional approach. It still has to be evaluated whether the usage of e-assessments for clocking the learning content, as it was used in 2012/2013, supports a higher sustainability of learning. The quality of the papers, which are written by students for the case study, were similar. It must be mentioned, however, that the overall quality of the papers was not always acceptable. As the level of personal responsibility rises, the higher are the requirements towards the respective learner in terms of self-organization. A change from a passive learner to a more active learner is necessary. This change can not just be supported by the lecturer, rather it has to be supported and accepted by the learners themselves.

6.6 References

Baker, James Wesley. 2000. The classroom flip. Using web course management tools to become the guide on the side. In: Chambers, J.A. (Ed.). Selected Papers from the 11th International Conference on College Teaching and Learning. Jacksonville, Florida. 9–17.

Erpenbeck, John/Sauter, Walter. 2007. Kompetenzentwicklung im Netz. New Blended Learning mit Web 2.0. Luchterhand in Wolters Kluwer Deutschland, Cologne.

Handke, Jürgen. 2013b. The VLC Video Strategy. In: Handke, Jürgen/Kiesler, Natalie/Wiemeyer, Leonie (Eds.). The Inverted Classroom Model. The 2nd German ICM-Conference –Proceedings. München: Oldenbourg. 59–76.

Hattie, John/Timperley, Helen. 2007. The Power of Feedback. In: Review of Educational Research 77 (1). 81–112.

4 In the evaluation of the fall semester 2012/2013 there have participated 39 of 49 students. In the second year there were 39 out of 53 students.

Kerres, Michael/Schmidt, Andreas. 2012. Zur Anatomie von Bologna-Studiengängen. Eine empirische Analyse von Modulhandbüchern. In: Kerres, Michael/Hanft, Anke/Wilkesmann,Uwe/Wolff-Benedik, Karola (Eds.). Studium 2020. Positionen und Perspektiven zum lebenslangen Lernen an Hochschulen. Munster: Waxmann. 82–97.

Lage, Maureen J./Platt, Glenn J./Treglia, Michael. 2000. Inverting the Classroom: A Gateway to Creating an Inclusive Learning Environment. In: The Journal of Economic Education 31 (1). 30-43.

Loviscach, Jörn. 2013.Videoerstellung für und Erfahrungen mit dem ICM. In: Handke, Jürgen/Sperl, Alexander (Eds.). Das Inverted Classroom Model – Begleitband zur ersten deutschen ICM-Konferenz. München: Oldenbourg. 25–37.

Slepcevic-Zach, Peter/Tafner, Georg. 2012. Input - Output - Outcome: Alle reden von Kompetenzorientierung, aber meinen alle dasselbe? Versuch einer Kategorisierung. In: Paechter, Manuela/Schmölzer-Eibinger, Sabine/Stock, Michaela/Slepcevic-Zach, Peter/Weirer, Wolfgang (Eds.). Handbuch Kompetenzorientierter Unterricht. Weinheim/Basel: Beltz. 27–41.

Schulmeister, Rolf/Metzger, Christiane. 2011. Die Workload im Bachelor. Ein empirisches Forschungsprojekt. In: Schulmeister, Rolf/Metzger, Christiane (Eds.). Die Workload im Bachelor Zeitbudget und Studierverhalten. Eine empirische Studie. Münster: Waxmann. 119.

Spannagel, Christian. 2011. Das aktive Plenum in Mathematikvorlesungen. In Berger, Lutz/ Grzega, Joachim/Spannagel, Christian (Eds.). Lernen durch Lehren im Fokus. Berichte von LdL-Einsteigern und LdL-Experten; ein Workshop-Band zum LdL-Tag 2009 an der Pädagogischen Hochschule Ludwigsburg. Berlin: epubli GmbH. 97–104.

Spannagel, Christian/Spannagel, Jana. 2013. Designing In-Class Activities in the Inverted Class room Model. In: Handke, Jürgen/Kiesler, Natalie/Wiemeyer, Leonie (Eds.). The Inverted Classroom Model. The 2nd German ICM-Conference – Proceedings. München: Oldenbourg. 113–121.

[INT 1] Gannod, Gerald C./Burge, Janet E./ Helmick, Michael T. 2007. Using the Inverted Classroom to Teach Software Engineering. In: Miami University - Technical Report (MU-SEAS-CSA-2007-001) 2007. http://sc.lib.muohio.edu/bitstream/handle/2374.MIA/206/fulltext.pdf, last accessed on 06/26/2014.

[INT 2] Kolmos, Anette/Du, Xiangyun/Holgaard, Jette. E./Jensen, Lars Peter. 2008. Facilitation in a PBL environment. http://vbn.aau.dk/files/16177510/Facilitation_in_a_PBL_envir onment.pdf; last accessed on 06/26/2014.

7 Blending Service Learning and E-Learning Elements in Higher Education: Experiences with a Variation of the *Inverted Classroom Model*

Philip Meyer

This report reflects on a course at the University of Augsburg, which I taught from April 2012 until February 2014 during my work for the initiative *"Bildung durch Verantwortung"* (Sporer et al., 2011: 72ff.). The course had been co-developed by the University of Augsburg and the FAU Nuremberg-Erlangen for Bavaria's virtual university network (Jahn/Meyer/Stitz, 2012). At the University of Augsburg, it is still collaboratively conducted by the chair of media didactics and the media lab (Mayrberger, 2014; Sporer, 2014). The course is entitled 'Service Learning: Social Learning in Schools, Universities and Further Education.' It is based on a blended learning concept and to my belief is very much related to the idea of ICM at its core. Though we never used the term ICM when we thought out the course, the goal was always to attain 'the best of both worlds,' which includes the online and face-to-face experiences. For the latter we decided to implement a *Service Learning Approach* (Sliwka/Frank, 2004), as coined by Sliwka, which seeks to foster students' civic responsibility so that learners not only read and hear about the service learning method but also make and reflect their own experiences with it in a pragmatic fashion (cf. Dewey, 1938). In terms of learning goals, we expected the students to gain pedagogical knowledge about service learning and to acquire personal and social competencies in their projects, also reflecting their own stance towards civic engagement.

7.1 Enriching *Service Learning* with digital media

Service Learning is a teaching concept which is not particularly 'high tech', rather it is *"high touch,"* as Zlotkowski (2008, XII) fittingly stated. In other words, you can hardly do service learning without letting students participate in real-world interaction with people in the local communities surrounding educational institutions. There exists a large network of teachers who do service learning completely without making use of digital media (cf. Stark/Buchholz/Badur, 2014) – and they do so successfully. Usually, they combine conventional classroom instruction and project work in non-profit community organizations (cf. Kielsmeyer, 2010, as cit. in INT 4). But there were two main reasons why we decided to switch to 'Service Learning 2.0' and these do not primarily concern the needs of the teacher but rather of the students. Firstly, students, to a large proportion, are 'online' and prepared to organize and work through learning materials at home. And secondly, students like to spend time participating in hands-on service learning projects, having an adequate and appropriate amount of workload assigned to them, i.e. a minimum 40 hours per semester (cf. Bartsch/Reiß, 2009: 50). As a consequence, we decided (1) to invert the knowledge dissemination, implementing it into an online learning environment and developing rich media content and (2) to create online and face-to-face spaces for communication, collaboration, and reflection of student projects.

7.2 Web-based dissemination of course relevant knowledge

In preparation for their service learning experiences, students worked through corresponding chapters of the online learning environment. They combined texts, images, filmed lectures and video expert interviews. The video lectures provided introductory information about the course topic and were meant as a starting point before diving deeper into the theoretical background of the concept. Furthermore, interviews with experts from all around Germany served the purpose of providing concrete examples of how service learning can be applied in teaching practice. Reading the text by given deadlines was obligatory, and understanding the text was a precondition for succeeding in subsequent graded exercises. Since we provided many hours of video, watching all of them completely was not considered a mandatory task. As a consequence, students tended to concentrate on the texts, also printing them out. Spannagel (2012) observed that it is difficult to adequately communicate the purpose of course videos to the students in a video-oriented flipped classroom scenario. This corresponds with our experience. Students tended to ask whether watching the videos was a 'must.' If merely optional, how can we justify the resource and time intensive production of video materials that students may rarely watch?

Figure 7.1: Left: filmed lectures embedded in the text; Right: expert video interviews (Jahn/Meyer/Stitz, 2012)

Judging by the performance on the course exercises and the results of evaluations, most students are getting along well with the texts and videos on the course topics. One reason for that might be that we structured the materials with reference to the stages of project work, which the students go through sequentially. For example, in the beginning students were confronted with the task of planning their service learning project. The texts offer them project management methods as well as theories of project-based learning and group formation processes, which can be helpful to them during that respective period. The same goes for all other stages of the service learning process. The classroom is inverted in the sense that after dealing with the online materials, student discussions and application of knowledge take place face-to-face during the student project group meetings, in the facilities of the local community partner, and in occasional classroom meetings which are held to share and reflect on the service learning experiences.

7.3 Web-based formation of student teams

In addition to knowledge dissemination, another process which conventionally happens in the physical classroom is the formation of student teams. After the team has been formed by the teacher, students meet at home, in the library or online to work on their projects. We decided to switch this process as well, as it is sometimes confusing (especially with big class sizes) to use face-to-face time for group formation. Also, service learning projects should meet both the interests of the students and of the partner organization in order to be successful, so one is advised not to rush through this phase. A four-step team formation process has repeatedly proven to be useful to support the composition of service learning teams in my course with 30 to 70 participants. Various forms of media were applied, using web technologies to support both the information dissemination and voting phases.

(1) **First Information Phase.** Already a few weeks before the beginning of the semester, we contacted many service learning partner organizations, who then sent in project idea forms which thoroughly described ideas for student projects. We then passed on information on project ideas to the students before the semester started by communicating them through the web.

(2) **First Voting Phase.** The students were now asked to give multiple unbinding votes on project ideas that sound generally interesting to them. A free online voting tool was suitable for supporting this step (e.g. *tricider.com*, see www.tricider.com/de/brainstorming/KEZK for an example service learning vote). The students were actively encouraged to give many votes for different ideas so that the broad interests were captured in this step. The voting via *tricider* or similar tools is (and should be) easily accessible, not requiring any registration or student data except from the student's name.

(3) **Second Information Phase.** In order to bring students and community partners together for the discussion of project ideas, the partner organizations with the most popular proposals were invited to the second course session to present their ideas in the classroom and answer questions on the project ideas. Also, even more informative material (see step 1) was now communicated to the students. The students got the chance to talk to each other about the projects and to socialize with potential team partners.

(4) **Second Voting Phase.** After the introductory classroom session was over the students were asked to adjust their project preferences in the online voting tool (see step 2) based on the presentations and discussions they had on that day. They were required to make final decisions regarding the choice of projects within the same week, and these decisions were binding. We then decided on the data basis of the two voting phases about the team composition. Our goal was to find the balance between a) enabling as many projects as possible and b) giving each student at least one of the projects he favoured in voting phase 1 or 2. With the help of the preference data it was easier to balance the individual interest of students and community partners.

The detailed group formation procedure is described in an article by Miller, Meyer and Ruda (2014). Though not every student got to work with the community partner organization they wanted to, satisfaction was generally high, also on the side of the partner organizations. We had exceptionally good experiences with letting students articulate which group members they desired and which projects were their top priorities.

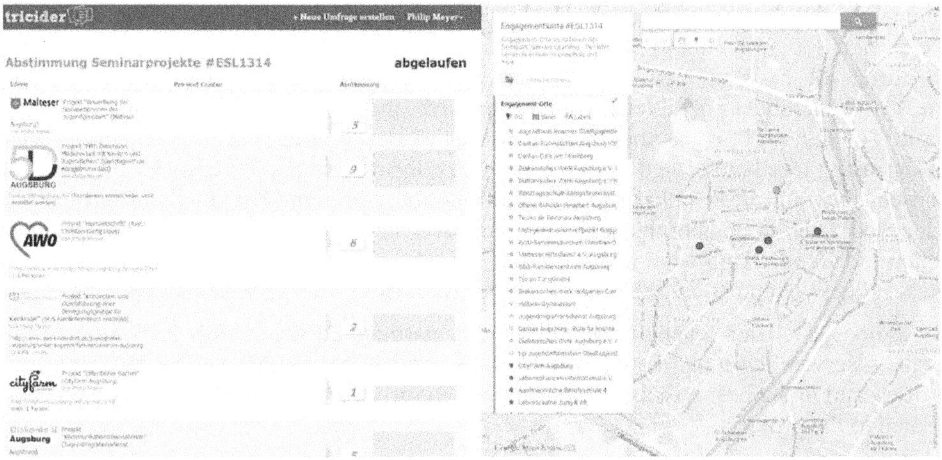

Figure 7.2: Left: Online voting with an overview of project ideas; Right: Student articulate their own ideas on a collaborative map

7.4 Supporting students face-to-face in Blended Service Learning

When the projects started, we as teachers joined the student teams for their first meeting with the community partner. The response to this was clearly positive and widely considered as a strong commitment from the teacher's side, as we did not treat the student service as mere practical work outside the academic world, but as an integral part of learning. For every project an appointment was scheduled in the facilities of the respective community partner. At least one employee of the community partner, one teacher and the majority of the students assigned to the project (approximately 1 to 5) were present. The community partner first outlined (again, after the information provided in front of the whole class) the idea for the students' service. For example, one group was advised to find ways to improve the public relations of their local board and care retirement home, so that in consequence more elderly people decide to move in. Afterwards, we brainstormed and discussed ideas for solving each particular problem. Last but not least I, as the teacher, then brought in the learning goals of the course, which were in this case that the students should gain pedagogical knowledge with special regards to media education. I also stressed that the students were not expected to work more than a fixed amount of hours and that I, as an educator, was interested in their learning process rather than the results of their respective projects. In our teaching through the initiative *"Bildung durch Verantwortung"* (Sporer et al., 2011) we usually put emphasis on the learning process, as we are aware that students are not necessarily to blame for the failure of their project. On the contrary, they can learn a lot from reflecting on project failure, as the following example demonstrates:

In January 2014 a student came to my office, asking for a consultation. She seemed very uncomfortable with the situation in her project. The community partner, a local women's movement, expected her and her (highly motivated) team to create an educational campaign on the topic 'lover boys', which is a form of sexual exploitation. Especially teenage girls are affected by the phenomena, when young men trap them into prostitution and drug abuse. While searching for empirical evidence apart from the many yellow press articles, she also talked to police officers and social science researchers on the topic. The bottom line was that there is no safe evidence of the phenomena being present in Germany; it rather seemed like a 'hype' and a form of fear-mongering by the media. In consequence and after talking to the disappointed community partner, the project was cancelled after three months upon my approval and the campaign never reached the schools, different from what had been planned. Nevertheless, the students later handed in great reflective reports and obviously learned a lot from what had been happening.

It becomes clear that teachers and community partners do not always fully agree on the goals in service learning. This is what makes service learning such a highly democratic process and in the best possible case everyone involved articulates their opinion on issues related to the projects.

In addition to meetings at the project start, we also scheduled several reflective sessions in class where students discussed their projects. Every group commented on their progress, so that the whole class was 'up-to-date'. We then split the groups into learning-tandems so that two persons who did not previously work together in a project got the chance to talk about their experiences and reflect on how there are related to the course topic. Questions we proposed for discussion included, for instance:

- *'What pedagogical competencies did I acquire in the project?'*
- *'To what extent is service learning sustainable?'*
- *'Can student efforts help to solve the community partner's problems in the long run?'*

The students were free to choose which one to discuss, which consequently led to an engaged debate in which many students participated. Still, the first question on pedagogical outcomes was not discarded as it was one that the students had to answer later on in their reflective reports.

7.5 Assessment of student learning

The assessment in the course has been divided into three distinct parts which differ regarding to their function for student learning. One third of the total course grade refers to the performance in the exercises related to the study materials. The aim of these aforementioned (see section 7.2) individual tests was to assess the learning goal of knowledge acquisition in the domain of service learning.

Another third of the final grade focused on the individual's competency development. Therefore, students were asked to keep a journal during their one-semester project. In this journal, students reflected on the salient events in their projects and tracked the workload they put into the projects. Several times during the semester they were expected to take the time to write down what happened in their projects and how they evaluated the course of the project work. This reflective process was scaffolded with guiding questions that were derived from Jones/Shelton (2006: 51):

Table 7.1: Scaffolding reflection-in-action through the guided journal (described in Sporer/Sippel/Meyer, 2010)

Time span	Objective Events / Activities	Subjective Impressions / Evaluations
01.04.13 until 07.04.13	**Step 1: Description of situation** What events have happened since the last journal entry (meetings, artefacts of work, etc.)? When and where did these events take place and what are their results for the project? Who participated in the events and what role did they take on in the project group? **Step 4: Projections and planning** Which future tasks and goals have been agreed upon and were co-ordinated between the group members? How do I assess the implications of these plannings for the prospective course of the project? What further changes do I want to achieve with respect to future work within the project?	**Step 2: Analysis and interpretation** What are my thoughts and feelings regarding the current situation of the work in the project? How do I evaluate this situation and the previous course of action in the project? Which opinions, premises, expec-tations influence my evaluation? **Step 3: Insights und implications** What chances and problems do I expect for the next steps in the project work? How do the events affect my motivation and the atmosphere in the project group? What are the consequences that I infer from my reflection on the current situation in the project?

The four steps of the reflective process illustrated in Table 7.1 instructed students to reflect-in-action and to observe their learning as a cyclic and iterative process (cf. Schön, 1987). They were aimed at teaching students to think about their experiences within the project in a systematic way. Students learned to separate the events that occurred in the project from their subjective impressions as well as how to evaluate the events from their personal point of view and to put them into relation with the course's learning goals. At the end of the semester the project journals were handed in for grading. The journals allowed for grading individual engagement and progress related to the course, yet it is difficult to be fully objective with what is written down. It is sometimes hard to tell the difference between 'nicely put words' and real engagement only from the journal entries, disregarding other aspects, such as classroom participation, e-mails or contact during office hours. It helped that I could resort to several assessment criteria which had been developed for the assessment of student learning outcomes (cf. Sporer/Sippel/Meyer, 2010).

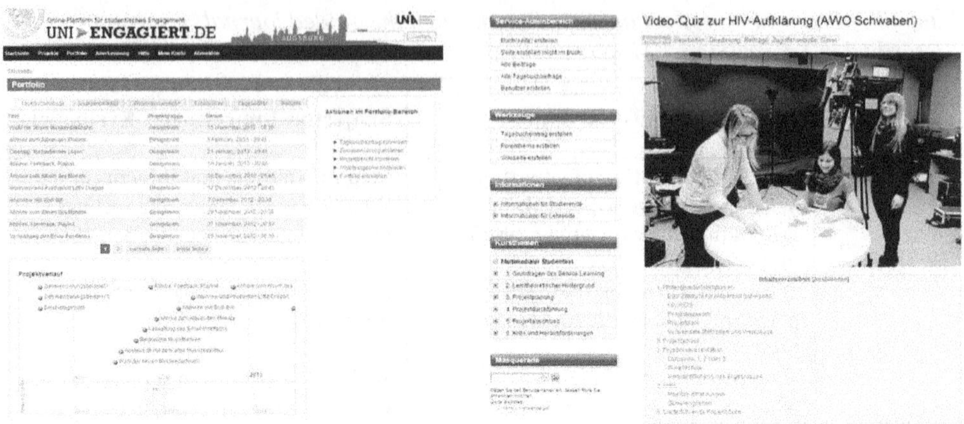

Figure 7.3: Left: A collection of student journal entries; Right: Example of a collaboratively constructed wiki (Jahn/Meyer/Stitz, 2012)

The last third of the total course grade was given for collaboratively constructed wikis. Each group worked on a *wiki* page for their respective project, containing sections regarding background information, project development, presentation of results, and a reflective section about lessons learned. The wikis were located within the Drupal-built learning management system of the course. During construction, they were labelled 'private' and could only be accessed by the students who worked on it. After finishing the *wiki* pages, the students and the community partner could decide whether they wanted the project information to be public or not. Most of the students decided to make their pages publicly visible (for a collection of wikis see http://tinyurl.com/n7dq9kw).

Besides mere publicity, the wiki served the main purpose of making the project result (e.g. a media product, workshop or pedagogical concept) part of the grading, yet not judging it directly. We found it more suitable to grade the learning process rather than the product, applying the portfolio method (cf. Häcker, 2004). There were three reasons for this decision, one being that projects can fail (see example in 4.4) with the consequence that products lose their relevance. Another reason was that the range of possible products and services is too wide to use comparable assessment criteria for all of them. It is hard to compare apples with oranges. Last but not least, the existing knowledge students possess about the course topics differs. Therefore, judging the product would not value individual progress. A recent example of learning scenarios with a similar or even more diverse audience is *Massive Open Online Courses* (Cormier/Siemens, 2010). The portfolio method might offer ways to assess and support this new form of learning in the future.

7.6 Conclusion

As outlined, service learning seeks to connect academic learning with a service for the common good. Its strengths lie especially in the fostering of social and personal competencies. Yet whether students also gain discipline-specific knowledge during their service learning project is debatable. Some might argue that you only apply and practice what you already know. With the idea of an inverted service learning approach it is possible to bring in relevant knowledge though web-based dissemination, implementing the first phase of the *Inverted Classroom* (cf. Handke/Sperl, 2012) into service learning scenarios. Engaged discussion, debate and reflection, i.e. important aspects of the second phase, in any case play an essential role in service learning approaches. Still I would argue that even in those face-to-face discussions teachers need to think of ways to raise the implicit knowledge of the student projects, providing opportunities to connect their experiences with the academic discourse. It is a difficult yet provoking task to get from the operative level to the level of thinking which involves new theories and discussions of ways to collectively tackle today's challenges.

7.7 References

Cormier, Dave/Siemens, George. 2010. Through the open door: Open courses as research, learning, and engagement. Educause, 45(4). 30–39.

Dewey, John. 1938. Experience and Education. New York: Macmillan Co.

Jones, Marianne/Shelton, Marilyn. 2006. Developing Your Portfolio: Enhancing Your Learning and Showing Your Stuff. New York & London: Routledge.

Häcker, Thomas. 2004. Mit Portfolios in Projekten expansiv lernen. In: Krause, Dörthe/Eyerer, Peter (eds.). 2004. Projektarbeit mit Ernstcharakter. Ein Handbuch für die Praxis der Aus- und Weiterbildung in Schule und Hochschule. Pfinztal: TheoPrax Stiftung, Fraunhofer Institut für Chemische Technologie. 212–227.

Handke, Jürgen/Sperl, Alexander (eds.). 2012. Das Inverted Classroom Model. Begleitband zur ersten deutschen ICM-Konferenz. München: Oldenbourg.

Miller, Jörg/Meyer, Philip/Ruda, Nadine. 2014. Patterns on Civic Engagement, Service Learning and Campus Community Partnerships from the Program for the Advancement of Service Learning and Social Responsibility of Universities. Proceedings of the 18th European Conference on Pattern Languages of Programs EuroPLoP'13 at Kloster Irsee in Bavaria, Germany

Schön, Donald A. 1987. Educating The Reflective Practitioner. Toward a New Design for Teaching and Learning. San Francisco: Jossey-Bass.

Sporer, Thomas/Eichert, Astrid/Brombach, Julia/Apffelstaedt, Miriam/Gnädig, Ralf/Starnecker, Alexander. 2011. Service Learning an Hochschulen: das Augsburger Modell. In: Köhler, Thomas/Neumann, Jörg (Eds.). Wissensgemeinschaften: Digitale Medien - Öffnung und Offenheit in Forschung und Lehre. Münster: Waxmann. 70–80.

Sporer, Thomas/Sippel, Silvia/Meyer, Philip. 2010. E-Portfolios als Assessment-Instrument im Augsburger „Begleitstudium Problemlösekompetenz". Zeitschrift für Medienpädagogik 18, 1–18.

Sliwka, Anne/Frank, Susanne. 2004. Service Learning. Verantwortung lernen in Schule und Gemeinde. Weinheim/Basel: Beltz.

Zlotkowski, Edward. 2008. Foreword. In: Dailey-Hebert, Amber/Donnelli-Sallee, Emily/ DiPadova-Stocks, Laurie N. (Eds.). Service-eLearning: Educating for Citizenship. Charlotte, NC: Information Age. 119–129.

[INT1] Bartsch, Gabriele/Reiß, Kristin. 2009. Do it! Learn it! Spread it! Praxisleitfaden Service Learning an Hochschulen. http://www.ekhg.de/downloads/Praxisleitfaden.pdf; last accessed on 12/05/2014.

[INT2] Jahn, Dirk/ Meyer, Philip/Stitz, Gerhard. 2012. Service Learning. Multimedialer Studientext zum Online-Kurs "Soziales Lernen in Schule, Hochschule und Weiterbildung". www.service.e-learning.imb-uni-augsburg.de; last accessed on 12/05/2014.

[INT3] Mayrberger, Kerstin. 2014. *Service Learning*. Kursprogramm SS14 der Virtuellen Hochschule Bayern (VHB). http://kurse.vhb.org/VHBPORTAL/ kursprogramm/ kursprogramm.jsp?kDetail=true&COURSEID=5520,59,731,1; last accessed on 12/05/2014.

[INT4] National Youth Leadership Council. 2010. Educators Embrace Service-Learning as a Strategy for Improving Learning. Press release. http://www.harris interactive.com/vault/Harris_Interactive_News_2010_03_25.pdf; last accessed on 12/05/2014.

[INT5] Spannagel, Christian. 2012. Weiterentwicklung meiner Flipped-Classroom-Vorlesungen. http://cspannagel.wordpress.com/2012/12/23/weiterentwicklung-meiner-flipped-classroom-vorlesungen/; last accessed on 12/05/2014.

[INT6] Sporer, Thomas. (2014). *Lehrveranstaltungen und Studienprogramme.* Projekt „Bildung durch Verantwortung". http://www.uni-augsburg.de/projekte/bildung-durch-verantwortung/lehrangebote/; last accessed on 12/05/2014.

[INT7] Stark, Wolfgang/ Buchholz, Detlev/Badur, Imke-Marie. 2014. Hochschulnetzwerk Bildung durch Verantwortung. http://www.netzwerk-bdv.de/; last accessed on 12/05/2014.

8 The *Inverted Classroom Model* in Law Studies

Oliver Kreutz, Himanshi Braun, Almut Reiners, Andreas Wiebe

8.1 Introduction

8.1.1 Initial situation

Developments in computer and media technology in the last decades have resulted in a high degree of digitalization in many areas of life. Education and research in universities can benefit particularly from this development (cf. Johnson, 2014; Hilgendorf, 2005: 365). By the application of the computerized possibilities, a better temporal and spatial availability of knowledge and also a better structure and organization of studies can be reached. Besides, the teachers can be relieved from their daily routines (cf. Eirich, 2005: 277f.).

E-Learning has established itself in different fields of studies. But in law studies the level of reservation in online-based teaching and learning methods is still high. The law faculties have only changed their structures to a minimal degree over the last centuries. Still, they are facing the fact that the conditions for their existence changed radically: higher numbers of applicants, low budgets and higher performance pressure have changed the educational environment (cf. Hoppe, 2004: 158 ff.). Universities have to reconsider their position strategically (cf. Hoppe, 2004: 161). Consequently, many changes regarding e-learning are implemented step by step.

Certain organizational, technical and legal conditions are required to establish learning innovations in higher education. Teachers have to be open-minded to face any challenges. Students should be provided enough space and flexibility for self-guided studying.

8.1.2 Previous use of new media in law studies

The usage of new media in law studies had been restricted to the upload of lecture notes into a learning management system (LMS). Due to the legal copyright and data protection issues, jurisprudence in particular uses new media hesitantly and regards technology-enhanced teaching as unscientific (cf. Eirich, 2005: 185; Hilgendorf, 2005: 366; Ranieri, 2001: 859f.).

8.1.3 Motivation and ambitions

The 'pilot project for integration of blended learning in the law studies' was performed in the winter semester 2013/2014 at the Georg-August-University Göttingen. The aim of the project[1] was to test the intense usage of e-learning elements in law studies in order to establish these elements in the curriculum. The project was performed in the course 'Media Law' which is part of the elective module ‘Public and Private Media Law'. It has a modular structure and covers a wide range of topics about media law.

The project not only aimed to implement e-learning elements in law studies but also to provide space for the application of innovative teaching and research methods in order to motivate the students to participate more actively. Therefore, the existing structure of the lecture was changed and enhanced with elements of blended learning. Students could still follow the learning content irrespective of location and time through an online media platform. Due to these changes of the course structure, the professor had more time in class to discuss other topics of media law and to develop higher teaching quality. Here, students were provided with time and chance to ask questions, repeat the content or discuss topics which were difficult to understand.

8.2 ICM in law studies

8.2.1 Concept design

The *Inverted Classroom* concept combines teacher-centered classroom training with elements of technology-enhanced and self-guided learning and inverts the traditional learning setting: content instruction takes place in classroom environment, the consolidation at home by self-instruction (cf. Keller, 1968; Schäfer, 2012).

The inversion from teacher-centered to self-guided learning has a number of advantages, such as:

- possibilities for students and teachers to discuss and reflect with each other,
- to solve individual comprehension difficulties,

[1] Funded by the BMBF (Federal Ministry of Education and Research) „Qualitätsprogramm für Lehre und Studium, Göttingen Campus Q[PLUS]" (Gemeinsames Bund-Länder-Programm für bessere Studienbedingungen und mehr Qualität in der Lehre. Dieses Vorhaben wird aus Mitteln des Bundesministeriums für Bildung und Forschung unter dem Förderkennzeichen 01PL11061 gefördert. Die Verantwortung für den Inhalt dieser Veröffentlichung liegt beim Autor.)

- to deepen knowledge,
- to integrate practical training, and
- to adjust the individual speed of learning.

Due to these potential advantages, this model seems to be the ideal solution to implement the requirements of the project.

The *Inverted Classroom Model* (ICM) was chosen to be implemented in the lecture 'Media Law' and aligned to the specifications of the course. The lecture is structured in three phases per week which offer a variety of learning methods. Students may choose from these methods to learn to accommodate their individual needs. As an example, students can learn with videos, podcasts or lecture notes to prepare for class. Furthermore, there are several synchronous and asynchronous methods for post-preparation and supervision such as an online discussion board and online meetings. Due to the variety of media-supported methods, free space for practical and competence-oriented learning was provided in presence phases and group work.

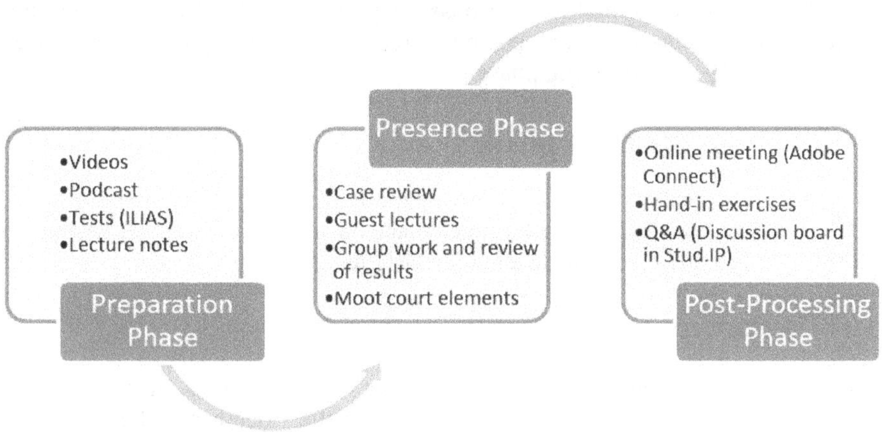

Figure 8.1: The three phases of a weekly schedule

8.2.2 Reorganization of content and structuring

The changed concept required redevelopment and restructuring of the initial content. The lecture with a common duration of 90 minutes was divided into sequences of 20-25 minutes, each serving one specific topic. The content was redesigned and adapted to the new format and transformed into new lecture notes and slides. Also, additional information and material (e.g. legal texts, judgments, and literature) was explored and edited for post-usage in the video lectures.

Furthermore, questions were made available as formative assessment (online tests in the learning content management system (LCMS) ILIAS) for each video sequence. The videos were recorded within a week's time of the semester break by Professor Wiebe. Additional material (scripts, ILIAS tests, case reviews, tasks for presentation etc.) was created and organized by the staff of chair. Because of the complete reorganization of the presence phase, plenty of time and personnel resources were needed. Law experts were recruited for guest lectures and group work had to be conceptualized. Professor Wiebe was equipped with a new staff member and various student assistants. Also, the e-learning service of the university supported this project with technical and didactical advice.

8.3 Weekly schedule

The weekly schedule of the class includes several elements of learning and knowledge transfer. In addition to the two basic phases of the *Inverted Classroom Model* (ICM; cf. Schäfer, 2012: 4), there is another third phase important for this learning environment. The concept of this course is divided into three phases – the preparation phase, the presence phase and post-processing phase.

8.3.1 The preparation phase

In this phase of a weekly class in a variety of the ICM, students are supposed to study independently. The knowledge transfer takes place on a self-guided level, whereas most of the content is provided from the teacher (cf. Schäfer, 2012: 4).

8.3.1.1 Lecture recording

The pre-structured content was recorded before the beginning of the class. The recordings consisted of the presentation of the lecture, the video and audio of the teacher and an alterable element.

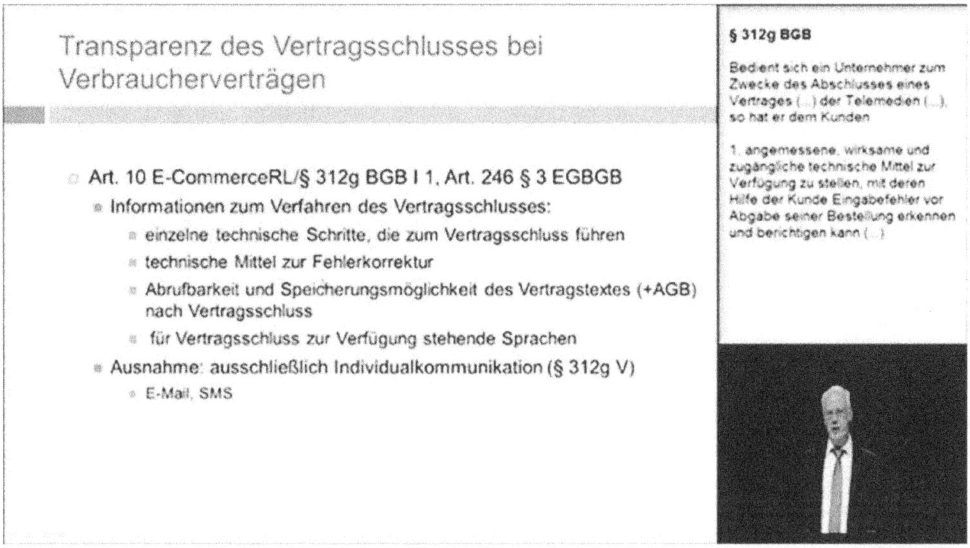

Figure 8.2: Screenshot of a lecture recording with three elements

The nature of this element was based on the content of the relevant slides and the discussed issue. Judgments, legal texts, contract clauses, bibliographical references, and other general explanations were adjusted to the video to provide more information about the respective topic.

The videos were recorded and edited with the screencasting software *Camtasia*. The software is ideal for changing and enhancing content in videos easily.

These lecture recordings could be accessed in a closed environment of the university internal LMS Stud.IP. Students were able to log in and stream the recordings at any place and any time, optionally with interruptions.

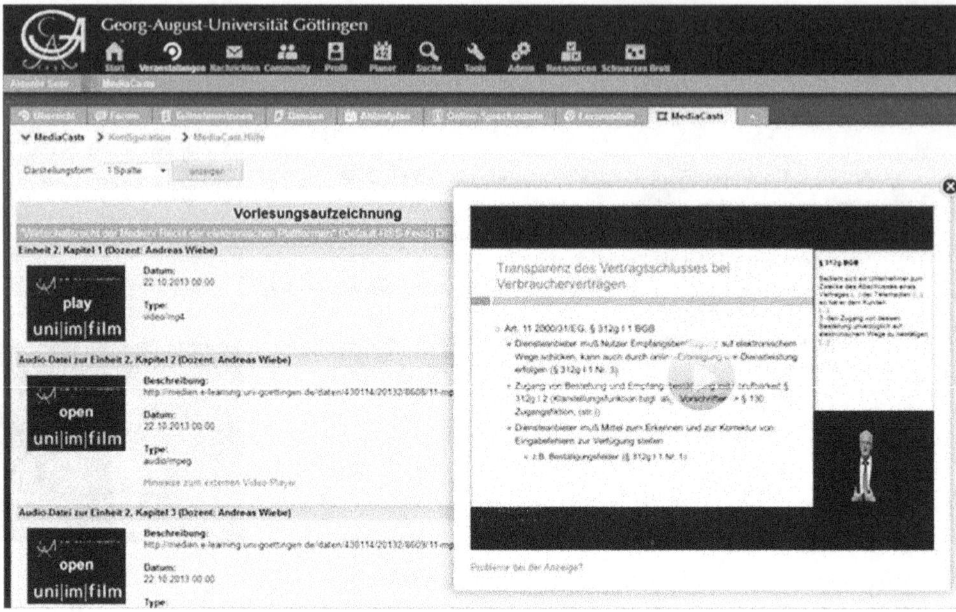

Figure 8.3: Integration of videos in the LMS Stud.IP

Supplementing the audio and visual presentation of the content, interactive whiteboards were used during the recording process for explaining complex issues. The use of such devices and their recording compensates for the use of a normal blackboard in classroom training.

To raise the attention of the students and to make them feel the classroom atmosphere, another aspect of in-class learning was simulated into the recorded environment. For this purpose, a group of staff members arranged a simulated student group and asked questions which were directly answered by the teacher. The other way around, the teacher asked questions into the plenum which were answered by the simulated group of students.

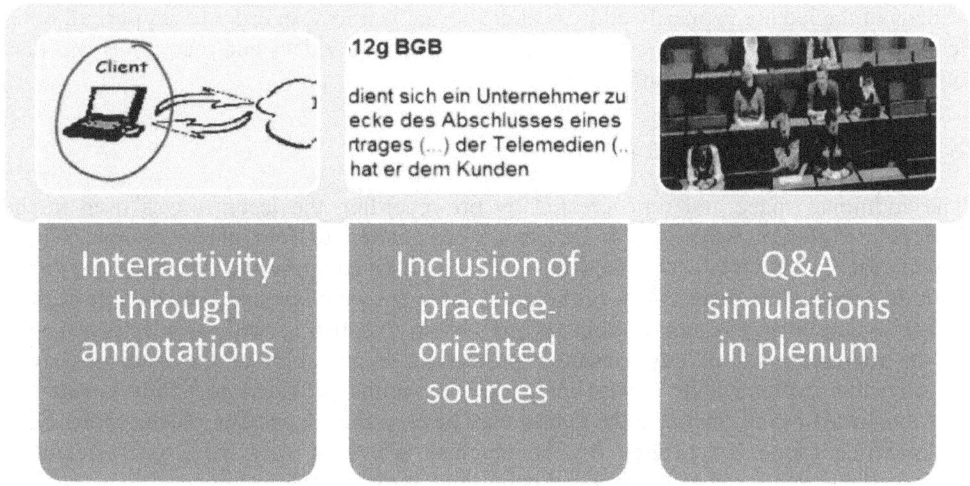

Figure 8.4: Tools to raise the interactivity in lecture recordings

8.3.1.2 Podcasting

The audio of the recordings was also provided for download and used outside of the learning management system. The format in use was MP3.

8.3.1.3 Formative assessment

The LCMS ILIAS enables tests for the self-guided preparation phase. The goal of these tests was the formative validation of self-instructed knowledge from the videos and lecture notes. The tests were aligned contextually to the video sequences.

ILIAS offers a variety of question types which can be used to verify knowledge. Besides single-choice and multiple-choice tasks, there are also image-map questions, cloze items (fill-in-the-blank texts) and matching exercises. Text-based topics were mainly acquired with single-choice and multiple-choice questions which were inserted in a test with a maximum of ten questions.

8.3.1.4 Learning material

Creating learning material for a scenario in such a variety of the ICM is different in comparison to the traditional paper-based classroom education. To supplement the lecture recordings with associated content, additional material was available for the students. When necessary, students could optionally use the supplementary material according to their individual thematic priority and focus of their studies.

In practice, students have to overcome certain obstacles to procure learning material, which is extremely time-consuming. Extensive bibliographical references directing learners to textbooks, commentary, judgments and other online sources were provided in a structured way corresponding to the relevant subject matter.

Videos of the lecture primarily address audio-visual learners. In order to support all other learner types, the material being discussed in the learning videos and recordings was also obtainable on the learning platform in textual form.

8.3.2 The presence phase

The additional space and time created by pre-recording the lectures was used in the project in different ways. Guest lecturers were invited to four class sessions. These experts each gave a talk about latest developments in media law and discussed the issues with the group of students. Most of the guest lecturers were lawyers. The data protection commissioner from the state of Schleswig-Holstein was also invited for a lecture as well as the representative of the consumer protection organization of the state of Lower Saxony. She explained the newest techniques of online providers to betray consumers and illustrated which fatal role the courts may have in these concerns. Such reports from the practice cannot be offered by the teachers which is why these guest lecturers provided interesting and relevant insights into the work of a media lawyer.

There was also successful group work arranged in the form of contract negotiations and judgment analysis. Students seemed to be highly motivated in this collaborative work environment and also improved their rhetorical skills. In a traditional law studies curriculum, there is only little space to improve soft skills. Another lecture included the creation of general terms and conditions for online business. The lecture was led by an IT lawyer. At the end of the lecture, the general terms and conditions created by the students were compared to a ones in use. In a further class. the very controversial UsedSoft Case of the Court of Justice of the European Union (C-128/11) was discussed and reenacted in a moot court. Both parties had the chance to prepare themselves through group work which was followed by a discussion and a 'judgment' of the court. To use the time of the presence phase meaningfully, students were encouraged to participate actively in the course, conduct a presentation and obtain credits or performance records.

8.3.3 The post-processing phase

8.3.3.1 Online meeting

Offering a satisfactory amount of support and personal supervision is important in law studies. Students should be able to discuss open questions and issues with their professors on a regular basis. Experience has shown that students are often open to asking comprehension questions if they can be anonymous and do not have to acknowledge their ignorance in public. Furthermore, this project also aimed at helping students gain training success by examining the content individually while benefiting from the professor's supervision.

An online meeting was offered once a week via *Adobe Connect*. The content of the week was provided during an online chat. Students were able to log in anonymously and ask or answer questions.

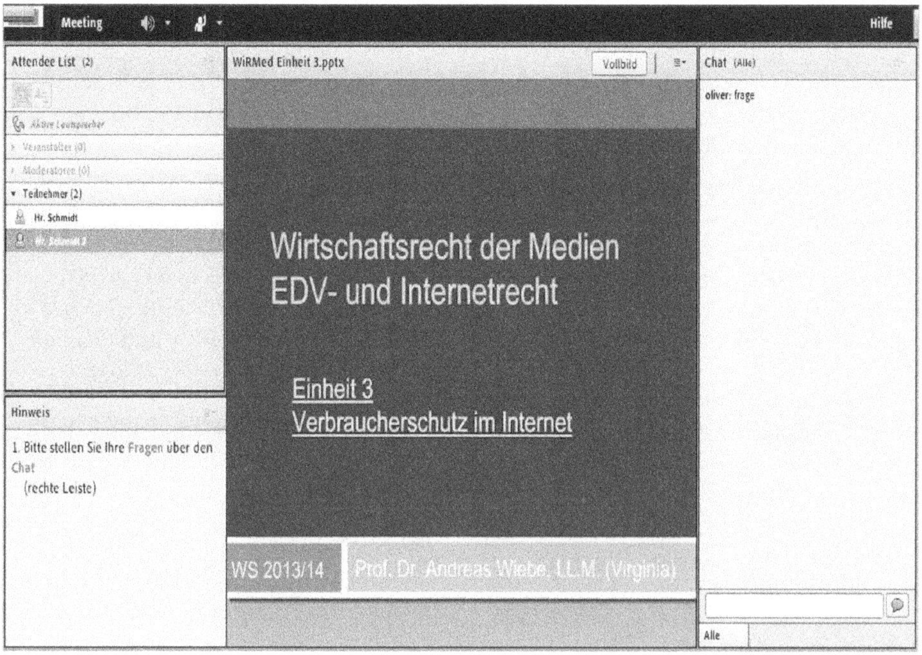

Figure 8.5: Screenshot of an Adobe Connect *online meeting*

8.3.3.2 Hand-in exercises

In this project, students had the chance to download online causes and hand in their individual solution via e-mail. The drafts of the students were corrected by a staff member.

8.3.3.3 Q&A in the Stud.IP discussion board

The inverted classroom concept was a challenge for participating students as they had to learn the content by themselves and purposefully use the media offered. To achieve excellent support and supervision the following actions were taken.

In addition to the in-class session and online meetings, students could get technical support in the discussion board of Stud.IP. These questions were answered within 24 hours by an advisor. Besides organizational and technical questions, students could also resolve contextual ambiguity issues. To support this, there were specific threads opened to discuss with other students and advisors. This communication method is asynchronous and can be used irrespective of the time of conversation.

8.4 Evaluation results

The project was evaluated as an online survey within two weeks at the end of the semester. It included 40 questions and the answers were based on a 5-level Likert Scale.

The survey was divided into three topics: 'general questions', 'questions regarding the project', and 'final improvements'. Finally, 40 of 67 participating students joined the survey (n=40). In the following section, only an excerpt of the survey will be represented, the complete survey may be found at http://www.uni-goettingen.de/de/118628.html.

The result of the survey showed that only a small fraction of students had already gathered experience with blended learning lectures. Only 15% of the students stated that they had had formal or informal contact with the concept of blended learning. The final result of the survey was evaluated positively: 100% of the participants said that the project was an interesting alternative to traditional lectures; 87% used the provided online materials on a regular basis. The video lecture was used by 95% and evaluated as very useful source by 62%, useful by 35% of the participants and only 3% declared the video material as less useful. Interpreting the access data, videos were commonly used before group phases in the in-class session. As a result, it can be concluded that team work increases the willingness to deal with the provided media and the formative assessment. Furthermore, 79% of all participants used the ILIAS tests.

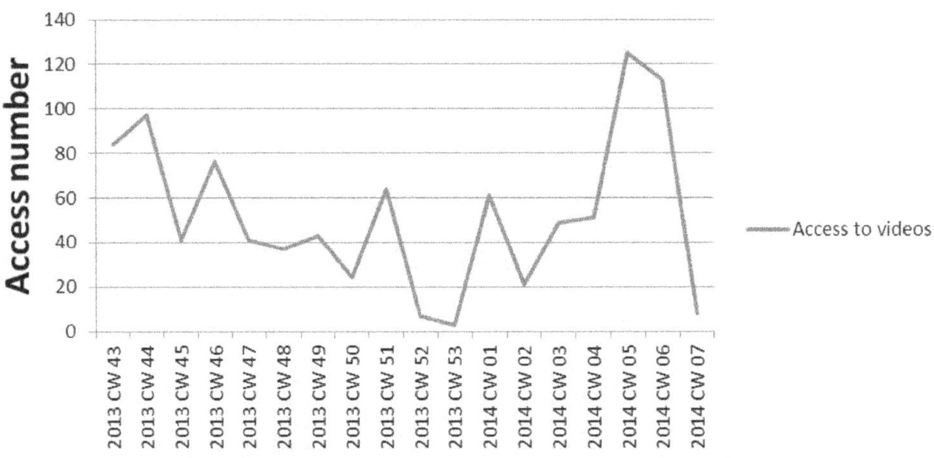

Figure 8.6: Usage of lecture recordings

The in-class phase was regularly visited by an average of 60% of the participants of the project. Those who visited the in-class session described the revised format as challenging, diversified and instructive. The vast majority of students desires more lectures in this format.

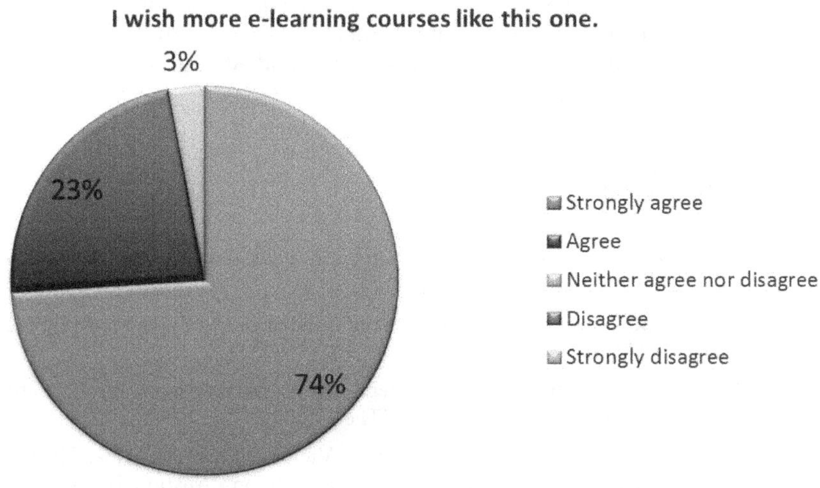

Figure 8.7: An example of the evaluation results

8.5 Conclusion and perspectives

The *Inverted Classroom Model* has been proven to be the ideal instrument for redesigning the course structure. The aim of this project was to gain more space for the teachers to develop and implement new teaching methods and provide the students more practice-oriented content.

In the preparation phase, students were encouraged to deal with the content of media law by themselves. They appreciated the concept of self-guided learning and accepted the challenge as well as the offered learning material (videos, podcasts, ILIAS tests, lecture notes, etc.) for the preparation of the class.

The transformed in-class phase enabled the development of soft skills such as rhetorical skills, collaborative learning, and negotiating skills. Beforehand, the students were subjectively experienced as passive listeners, but throughout the course their transition to active participants was obvious. Lectures with practical relevance seemed to be valuable for law studies, as most of the students join law practice at the end of their studies. The number of graduates adopting an academic career is considerably less.

In the post-processing phase, there was a slight difference in the acceptance of the offered possibilities. For example, the online meetings were only visited in the first weeks from a nominal number of participants. On the one hand, a reason for the rejection could be the existing possibility to ask questions and discuss open issues in the presence phase. On the other hand, students indicated lack of time and increasing amount of work as further causes.

In conclusion, the ICM will continue to be the basis for the teaching model applied in the course 'Media Law', but in an adapted way, where the supervision in the post-processing phase will be reduced. Moreover, the chair of Professor Wiebe and the e-learning service of the university are working to motivate and support further law teachers and chair holders to implement single e-learning elements in their lectures. These proceedings are desired by 100% of all participating students and should therefore be regarded as decisive for future teachings.

8.6 References

Eirich, Karsten. 2005. E-Learning in der juristischen Ausbildung. In: Juristische Ausbildung (JURA) 2005. 277–284.

Hilgendorf, Eric. 2005. Juristenausbildung und neue Medien. In: Juristenzeitung (JZ) 2005. 365–373.

Hoppe, Gabriela. 2005. Entwicklungen strategischer Einsatzkonzepte für E-Learning in Hochschulen. Lohmar (u.a.): EulThe.

Johnson, Larry/Adams Becker, Samantha/Estrada, Victoria/ Freeman, Alex. 2014. NMC Horizon Report: 2014 Higher Education Edition. Austin, Texas: The New Media Consortium.

Keller, Fred S. 1968. Good-bye, teacher... Journal of Applied Behavior Analysis, 1(1), 79–89. doi:10.1901/jaba.1968.1–79

Ranieri, Filippo. 2001. Der Computer, mein Repetitor – Die Neuen Medien und die neuen Verwirrungen in der deutschen Juristenausbildung. In: Juristenzeitung (JZ) 2001. 856–861.

Schäfer, Anna Maria. 2012. Das Inverted Classroom Model. In: Handke, Jürgen/Sperl, Alexander (eds.). 2012. Das Inverted Classroom Model. Begleitband zur ersten deutschen ICM-Konferenz. München: Oldenbourg. 3–12.

IV Implementation of the ICM in High School

In his talk at the 2014 ICM conference, Dirk Weidmann demonstrated that implementing the *Inverted Classoom Model* in high schools can be of great benefit to learners and teachers. The English-as-a-foreign-language (EFL) classroom can be enhanced by his variation of the model, as explained in his article in this volume. In his project with his grade seven English language class, the learners not only participated in every planning step but also developed their own teaching materials, i.e. learning videos. With the evaluation of his teaching scenario, Weidmann demonstrates that implementing the ICM in high schools provides an opportunity to activate learners, to increase individualized learning, and to develop key competences.

9 Increasing Learner Activity in the First ICMM Phase: a First-Hand Report

Dirk Weidmann

9.1 Introduction

In the realm of competence-based teaching, teachers are constantly facing the challenge of offering a stimulating learning environment, thereby adjusting instructions as well as exercises towards their pupils' needs. Therefore, a profound diagnosis of the learners' language competences – based on a reliable amount of collected data – must be recognized as an indispensable prerequisite for establishing an effective learning route. According to Marianne Horstkemper (2006: 4), the results of this initial evaluation usually reveal a complex heterogeneity of the group and imply the necessity of a thorough and ideally individualized training which may pave the way for successful learning. However, John Hattie's findings (2009: 173–178) indicate that in addition to this first support students should be offered regular possibilities for self-evaluation as well as a great amount of concrete feedback. Both aspects are said to be indispensable to guarantee not only short-term, but also long-term advancement. Yet, with reference to Horstkemper (2006: 5), it is important to emphasize the fact that the underlying diagnostic investigations have to be classified as process diagnostics: although clearly error-focused, they do explicitly not strive for selection and grading. Hence, from the perspective of a teacher who emerges as an activator or facilitator, the consequences drawn from these insights have to be a permanent circle of (follow-up) diagnoses and preferably individualizing adjustments of scaffolding.

Against this backdrop, this article's aim is to shed light on the question of how individualized learning based on initial diagnostics can be enhanced even within the first phase of the ICMM learning environment. In this context, the underlying concept is to maintain the basic ICMM structure consisting of (1) knowledge acquisition, (2) formative assessment, and (3) in-class exercises while enriching this setting with selected learning by teaching elements. As a result, the learning scenario surpasses traditional ICMM settings in terms of the degree of learner activation, since students are asked to develop the ICMM material as, for instance, videos or short online-tests themselves. Even though the project discussed in this article has been planned for an EFL classroom and primarily intends to foster the pupils' language competence it seems nonetheless possible to transfer this idea to other topics, tasks, and school subjects.

9.2 Basic information about the pupils and the setting

In the project at hand, a group consisting of 22 pupils (11 male, 11 female) aged 12 to 14 took part. They all attended class 7 of an integrated secondary school in Hesse, with English being their first foreign language which they had up to this point learned for about two and a half years. Before the project had been started, the general learning atmosphere had benefitted immensely from a very polite tone, which also prevailed during the ICMM-based project. Concerning the pupils' level of language competence, several tests hinted at a broad heterogeneity. At the beginning of the term, for instance, an online test indicated that the majority of pupils had already achieved an adequate level of competence in the fields of listening and reading comprehension. Despite these promising results, however, the test also revealed some gaps in the areas of language awareness and grammar, in comparison to the curricula.[1] Based on the results of a semi-guided writing task, which the pupils had carried out without subsequent grading, most students had arrived at an elementary use of language in the domain of written production. Since class members had predominantly produced isolated sentences without linking words or other attempts to establish logical cohesion, their written performances had to be classified among the interim phase between the *CEFR* levels A1 and A2.[2] As a rare exception, only one girl had already mastered the requirements of the A2+ level.

In order to meet the needs of the learners while referring to the guidelines of the curricula, a competence-based teaching unit was designed to combine the school term's topics 'Great Britain' and 'sports' with the introduction to and practice of report writing. Furthermore, in addition to fostering their media as well as social competence, this unit was especially intended to contribute to enhance the learners' language competence. In order to offer both adequate repetition as well as stimulating exercises for the relevant grammar topics, lessons were designed to incorporate ICMM components. The methodology underlying the entire teaching unit was based on the learning route scheme introduced by Steveker (2011) and Leupold (2008). Since a profound reasoning in favor of this concept has been offered in an earlier book chapter,[3] this contribution leaves aside any further discussion of this aspect in order to focus on the project itself. Nonetheless, the structure of the learning route is presented in Figure 9.1 in order to offer a basic

---

1 See [INT 1].

2 With respect to the A1- and A2-subdefinitions for "overall written production", see [INT 2]: 23. The A1-definition reads as follows: *"[The learner] [c]an write simple isolated phrases and sentences." By implementing sentence connectives, the next level can be reached: "[The learner] [c]an write a series of simple phrases and sentences linked with simple connectors like 'and', 'but' and 'because'."*

3 See Weidmann (2013).

overview about the learning task. For the sake of clarity, those elements relying on ICMM components have been framed in red.

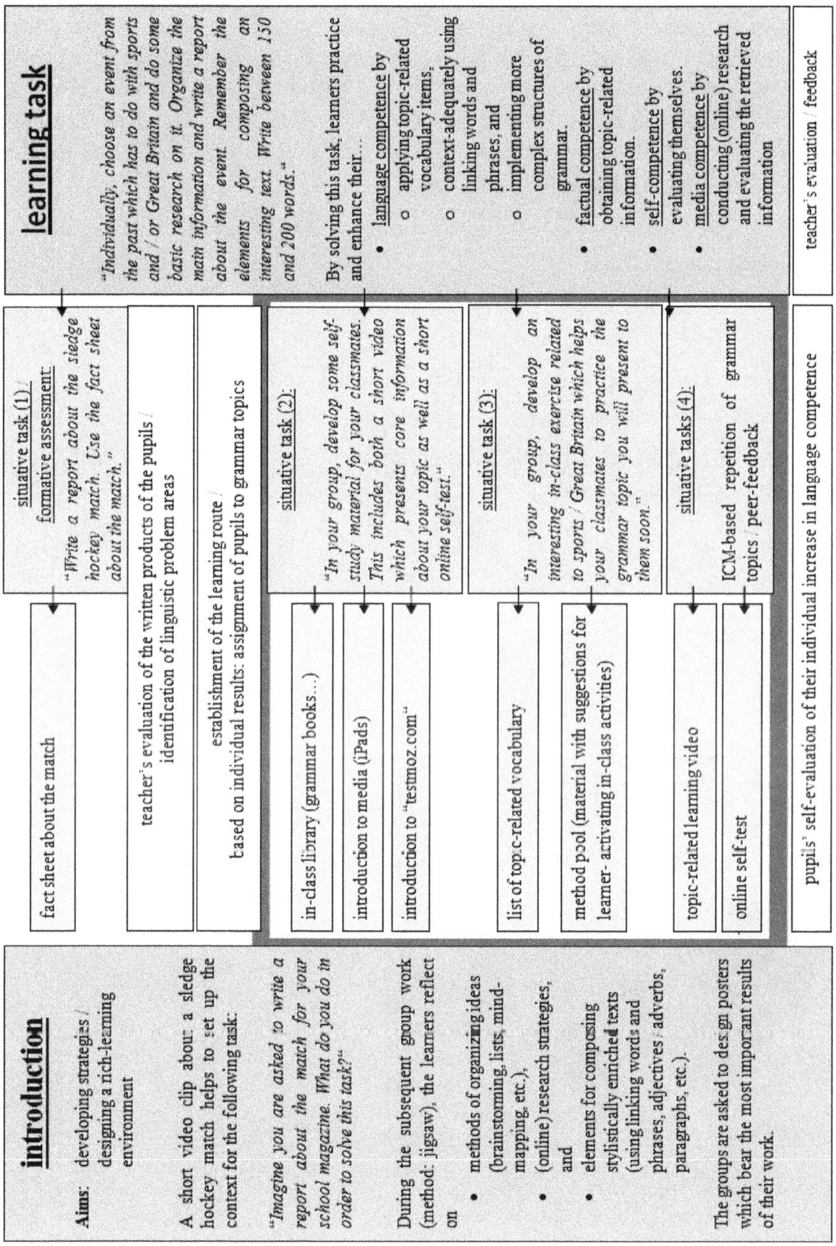

Figure 9.1: Teaching unit's underlying learning route as introduced by Weidmann (2013:168)

Having started the learning route by presenting parts of a sledge-hockey match on *YouTube* to the pupils as thematic introduction, it appeared to be essential from a teacher's perspective to identify those fields of grammar which tended to be most problematic for the pupils. The aim was to offer specific support so that pupils would ideally be able to master their problematic fields. Hence, all learners were asked to hand in a report on the short video sequence watched in class. A fact sheet distributed to the pupils helped to accomplish this task. Even though not graded, their texts were corrected and analyzed by the teacher and a set of comprehensive statistics was built up, systematically classifying all of the students' mistakes.[4] Ultimately, the following five areas turned out to be difficult for a lot of learners:

- orthography
- temporal subordinate clauses
- passive voice
- indirect speech
- distinction of adjectives / adverbs (incl. comparison)

Figure 9.2 offers a pie chart illustrating the percentage distribution of the problematic fields in the realm of language learning:

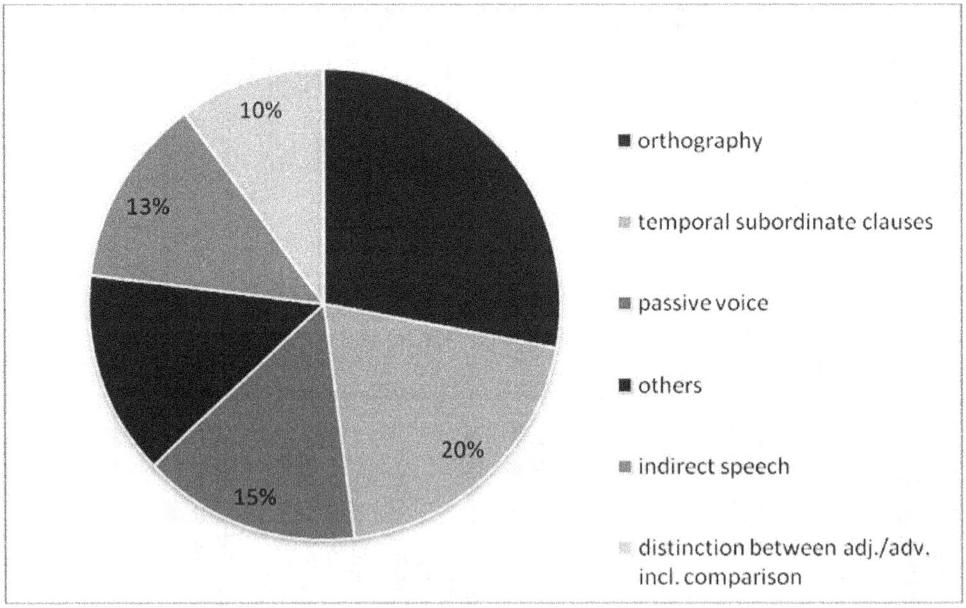

Figure 9.2: Teaching unit's initial error analysis.

[4] The weighting of mistakes follows the official guidelines offered in the *Oberstufen- und Abiturverordnung* (= [INT 3]: 93).

Although orthography had been identified as the most problematic domain, an ample treatment of this area during school lessons was postponed due to the fact that spelling mistakes are normally too individual to be tackled collectively in class. Instead, individualized strategies and exercises were offered for homework.[5] Besides this major domain of mistakes, certain types of grammar mistakes reoccurred in many of the students' texts. Among others, the tendency to overgeneralize the simple past suffix {-ed} was relatively common – a phenomenon which is said to not be uncommon among German learners of English as a foreign language.[6] All mistakes subsumed under the headline 'grammar mistakes' together contributed significantly to the average index of mistakes (= 6.9), so that fostering these fields was prioritized over common orthography exercises. When taking into account criteria for academic writing,[7] the future importance of both passive voice and reported speech cannot be overestimated, since students should obtain a wide range of linguistic abilities to express themselves trenchantly rich in variety. But even at this early point in their second language acquisition, however, the correct application of these structures would be beneficial for the learners due to the fact that a convincing report is based on a rather descriptive language. Therefore, advancing the students' competences in the aforementioned areas of grammar was already expedient to the upcoming tasks they had to fulfill.

9.3 The development of self-study material

Due to the fast pace and the multifacetedness of modern information processing, our schools have to face the challenge of preparing learners for an adequate approach towards media by systematically enhancing their media literacy. In this context, a core matter of interest should be to make students familiar with methods of how to rely on appropriate media tools for solving assigned tasks. By using media deliberately, pupils could act contrary to an alarming tendency referred to by Hasebrink/Lambert (2011: 4), according to which new media are only seldomly employed for learning purposes by teenagers.[8] Whenever opting for an opposite effect teachers will have to keep such tendencies in mind.[9]

Against this backdrop, the learning task at hand offered a unique chance: For the first phase of a traditional ICMM environment, the teacher normally either develops his own

5 Orthography problems mainly occur in the domain of words with weak phoneme-grapheme-correspondence. In order to face those individual problems, all learners were familiarized with a method called "sight word training", first introduced by Gerlach (2012).

6 See Ambridge/Lieven (2011: 255f).

7 See the criteria and statistics offered by Leech at al. (2005: 167f).

8 According to recent investigations in Germany carried out for the *JIM-Studie 2013* (= [INT 4]: 30–33), teenagers mostly go online for reasons of freetime communication through social networks, entertainment, and gaming. Manfred Spitzer (2012) has hinted at problems arising from this tendency, even though they may be overstated in the eyes of others. For a critical comment on Spitzer's assumptions, see exemplarily Bartens (2012).

9 See Weidmann (2012: 60–66).

material or brings in material conceptualized by others.[10] With respect to teaching videos, which have by now been accepted as a popular source of information in an ICMM-setting, Loviscach (2012: 32f) points to the special didactic needs required for successful ICMM-based learning.[11] For the learning route discussed in this article, however, the established ICMM concept has undergone a modification in this important part since the pupils were asked to develop learning material for their classmates themselves. In order to successfully master this task, the pupils first processed the assigned topics individually as well as in small groups. As a next step, they had to create a concept for a short, yet creative learning video to explain their grammar topic. According to Handke/Schäfer (2012: 86–92), videos address more than just one of the human senses, which is seen as a clear advantage in comparison to other possible teaching material such as worksheets, books or podcasts. Afterwards, they set out to produce the video by using tablet-PCs available at school. For the videos, it was vital to illustrate both the use and the formation of their respective grammar structures by presenting their own examples. As a consequence, all learners were finally able to rely on material offered by their classmates to prepare the contents during the first phase of the ICMM-based lessons. This way, all learners were positively dependent on each other and gained responsibility for the learning success of their peers since they were actively involved in the process of developing instructional material. To formally arrive at what has been coined *mastery learning*[12], the challenge to additionally designing media-based interactive exercises further enhanced the degree of learner activation in this first phase of the ICMM: students were given the chance to demonstrate mastery of the respective content at home before entering in-class exercises and discussions. This is why all pupils could expect an early comprehensive feedback on their learning progress.[13] Consequently, pupils might be advised during an early stage to review the videos or to fall back on different resources to familiarize themselves with the assigned content.

To begin with, students were asked to form small groups based on the results of the initial diagnosis indicating their major learning needs.[14] In order to join the most appropriate group, students were invited to enter into a dialogue with the teacher in

---

[10] See Schäfer (2012: 6f).

[11] If trying to come up with a motto underlying the videos of Jörn Loviscach, this could be "Keep it concrete and not too abstract." Loviscach (2012: 32), professor of mathematics at the University of Applied Sciences, describes the characteristic features of his videos as follows: "Der Stil ist betont anschaulich, visuell und deduktiv. Die Mathematik-Videos zeigen anstelle einer professionellen Formel mit Summenzeichen, Variablen und Indizes oft ein konkretes Beispiel, an dem man denselben Sachverhalt ohne den Ballast der Abstraktion erkennen kann. [...] Plausible Überlegungen ersetzen den formalen Beweis."

[12] For a first theory on what is called *Mastery Learning*, see Bloom (1971). With reference to the general structures of the ICM, Handke (2013) harked back to this concept to create the ICMM concept.

[13] For comprehensive remarks on the role of formative assessment, see Hattie (2009: 170–171). A recent study carried out by Schacter/Szpunar ([INT 5]) provides further evidence for the importance of early feedback when learning with computer and film-based material.

[14] The teacher consequently avoided the term 'expert groups' due to the critical remarks offered by Krumbach-Mollenhauer/Lehment (2010: 291) even though the term is quite popular among teachers, as Niggli (2001) has found out earlier.

addition to checking his written feedback on their written products. Due to this way of group allocation, the usual team-formations were split up, and many students had to cope with the challenge of cooperating with pupils with whom they had only rarely teamed up before. The number of students forming a group did not exceed six persons – however, groups with more than three members were asked to divide into two sub-teams in order to tackle different dimensions of their common topic.

As a next step, the second situative learning task had to be mastered.[15] Here, the student teams had to develop both a short video which presented core information about their topic as well as a corresponding short online self-test. Consequently, all course members could rely on self-study material after having planned and realized these tasks and sub-tasks within ten school lessons. As a first step, pupils had to familiarize themselves with the grammar topic at stake. Hence, they were encouraged to individually do research on their topic within an appointed period of time. In this context, the teacher offered a wide range of material as an in-class library (e.g. grammar books, encyclopediae, dictionaries, etc.), in the aggregate offering what Neuman (2011: 17–34) has referred to as a *rich learning environment*. Since the teacher had also provided differentiating material and an individualized amount of personal support in accordance with the pupils' needs, the concept was designed to ensure that each student could achieve individual progress while simultaneously contributing to the upcoming product of his or her team. Besides, learners were allowed to rely on five computer workstations for any purpose contributing to their aims. Here, students were eager to use them as a dictionary to look up unknown vocabulary, whereas these electronic devices were not consulted for carrying out further research on their topic – the pupils clearly preferred print material as the primary source. Later, they also made use of the PCs to exchange results within their groups by attaching drafts and products to emails or by sharing them with their classmates, respectively.

Having finished the individual process of knowledge acquisition, all group members exchanged their findings within their teams.[16] Consequently, each team could both arrive at a common understanding of their topic by clarifying questions and uncertainties as well as make arrangements concerning the allocation of the upcoming task. In order to challenge the students' ability of self-organization, all groups were requested to seek solutions self-dependently first: the teacher should only be consulted for feedback after the students have arrived at their own common position or suggestion. In general, problems were very rare and mostly of linguistic nature stemming from imprecise contributions or explanations of some group members. In this case, then, other team members asked them to paraphrase the thought – a tactic which mostly led to the desired success.

After having compared and finally drafted their ideas for the videos, the teams dedicated themselves to the production of the topic-related videos and the online self-test. In accordance with the stipulations framed within previous in-class discussions, the student teams were striving for videos that would also be interesting to watch and easy to remember due to a striking plot or appealing design. These criteria emerged from the assumption of the class that videos featuring these aspects would contribute more effectively to the memorization of their content. In accordance with the theory offered by

[15] For further information, see figure 9.1 given earlier in this article.

[16] For the importance of the underlying concept of peer-tutoring, see Hattie (2009: 79).

Handke/Schäfer (2012: 86–92), such videos induce an increased efficiency if compared to traditional media such as handouts, books, or podcasts. In addition, the vast majority of the pupils took it for granted that all benefits emerging from an unusual way of presentation would clearly outweigh the risk of distracting the students' attention from the content. In retrospect, three concepts emerged to be particularly creative. One team invented a short role-play which was intended to mirror a school scene. Here, an English teacher met one of his pupils and the pupil's father during a counseling session and finally set out to illustrate the basic rules of reported speech for the rather dumb parent, including the changes of pronouns and adverbs as well as the backshift of tense. Two other groups agreed on integrating *Playmobil* figures for short clips in order to compare various past tenses. As an example, one group prepared the model of a living room where a little girl was watching TV when her mother came back from a trip. Here, the content was visualized before they started to explain the underlying rules of grammar.

In order to realize the upcoming step, the class met in a special project room big enough to combine an individualized learning space with a PC lab. After having balanced the pros and cons, the teacher had finally decided to make use of the school's *iPad* 4 tablets for producing the videos.[17] The reason for this was the fact that their handling can be learned rather intuitively. In addition, tablets offer a wide range of possibilities in terms of modifying the clips thanks to available apps. Owing to this technology, then, the pupils could effectively work with a single electronic device for this part of the teaching unit, thereby leaving aside the necessity to transfer vast amounts of data to other PCs or to make themselves familiar with complex video editing programs. In this context, however, it is also important to lay emphasis on the fact that almost all learners were inexperienced with the handling of tablets: in their previous school career, they had not been in touch with this sort of media. Therefore, it was inevitable to invest some time in introducing the students to the possibilities and pitfalls of tablets prior to filming. Only three learners had indicated that a tablet was available at their parents' home, so that these pupils could rely on basic knowledge in terms of handling. Nonetheless, they stressed that they had hitherto only used their parents' tablets to play games, to realize web 1.0 applications (above all emailing), or to read e-books, but they had never used tablets as a tool for producing videos or logging something by camera before. Hence, the teacher demonstrated basic functions of *iPads* while projecting his own *iPad's* desktop with the help of a data projector and an *Apple TV*.

For cutting and further preparations of the video clips, the teams gained support by older pupils who were participants of one of the school's optional media courses and who had been invited to join the project for two lessons. The older pupils had prepared another short presentation which shed light on fundamental functions of a video editing app called *Pinnacle Studio.* Again, the tablet proved to be an adequate all in one tool for school purposes since all teams were ready to use this app confidently soon. Due to the integration of more experienced pupils into the project, yet another learning-by-teaching component was realized. After all, five school lessons were spent on preparing the videos. This amount of time turned out to be adequate since all pupils remained actively

[17] A comprehensive collection of arguments with respect to a possible in-class usage of tablets is offered online on the homepage of the *Medienberatung NRW* (= [INT 6]).

involved in the process and contributed to the constant modification and improvement of the video scripts, the video production, as well as the final video editing.

In order to implement the previously mentioned *mastery learning* concept, the generation of online self-tests was selected as further self-study material. In order to ensure an appropriate preparation for in-class exercises, the material had to be tackled mandatorily after having watched a video at home. The teams worked out several test formats including, for instance, Q&A tests, gap filling exercises, and multiple-choice tests. The class had agreed on these formats because they were comparatively easy to prepare and would not take too much time in practice. Bearing in mind these considerations, the teacher had decided to introduce the online test-generator *testmoz.com* as a working space. After all, there were three main reasons for drawing back on this online tool: (I) usage is free of charge, (II) access is possible without giving away sensible data such as private email addresses, and (III) users are guided through the process of establishing their own tests by means of clear menu navigation and simple menu hierarchy. Moreover, administrators have the chance to analyze a statistic displaying the users' overall achievements. In case that a lot of learners failed to master the relevant content after their first online self-check, special follow-up tasks and exercises could be designed by either the teacher or the responsible team to support the learners on their way of mastering the topic. Hence, this kind of online learning environment contributes to set up further in-class learning scenarios.

After having prepared a set of possible test questions at home and being introduced to this web tool, the teams soon agreed on a couple of adequate questions and offered ready-to-go online tests within one further school lesson.[18] In most cases, the teams preferred multiple-choice questions or gap filling activities to more complex test formats since this format led to a quick indication of the pupils' learning progress. As soon as both the videos and the online tests were ready, the teams were asked to share their products with the teacher, either via email or – most likely in case of a bigger file size – via memory stick. While all pupils were busy developing in-class exercises for the second phase of the ICMM-scenario, it remained to the teacher to bring together the entire amount of data on a DVD and to copy it for each member of the class. Besides the videos, the data storage device also covered a PDF file containing the links to all online self-tests. At this point, another positive side effect of this project can be highlighted: the majority of those pupils contributing to the project (= 75%) rely on the material as a source of reference down to the present day as they have indicated in a current investigation. These findings may lay further emphasis on the long-lasting effects, which originated from this project which will also be discussed at the end of this article.

The distribution of the DVD copies to each course member marked the end of the preparation of the self-study material and simultaneously smoothed the way for the various ICMM units covering all grammar topics at stake. Each of those units started with a short homework task to enter the first phase of the ICMM: the pupils were asked to watch the relevant video and to take the related online self-test. In the case that 20% or more of all questions were answered wrong, it was highly recommended to watch the video once again and to retake the test. The reason for giving this task for homework was the anticipated risk that various students might face the necessity of watching the

[18] An example for a student team's online self-test is provided under [INT 7].

assigned video several times before having mastered its content, so that the homework was intended to ideally lead all pupils to common grounds for further in-class activities. Interestingly, only three students had to watch a video twice on average. When entering the second ICMM phase, all students had the chance to raise concrete questions about the content of the videos. By doing so, they were enabled to further clarify the content, and the expert teams were more than happy to answer the questions. Afterwards, the rules were transferred into practice since the teams had introduced stimulating activities covering a variety of class arrangements and formats, thematically related to Great Britain and / or sports.

Due to a final writing task, all class members could demonstrate their increase in language competence. Each learner was requested to compose a report on an individually chosen sports event using between 150 and 200 words. Again, the teacher analyzed their products in terms of language and style and offered concise individual feedback with the help of a comprehensive feedback sheet. With reference to their written competence, all pupils had by now arrived at the A2 level of the *CEFR*. Almost half of the group had even achieved the A2+ level, and 5 learners were even ready to fulfill parts of the B1 level, since they managed to describe an event coherently. In total, the average mistake quotient could be reduced to 4.8%, a decrease of 2.1%. The weakest learner was even able to lower his mistake quotient by 3.3%. Most importantly, the number of mistakes was reduced in all of those areas which had been subject to training. The most significant improvement was realized in the domain of temporal subordinate clauses where about 50% fewer mistakes occurred. Fig. 3 offers a concise overview about the results of this final competence test.

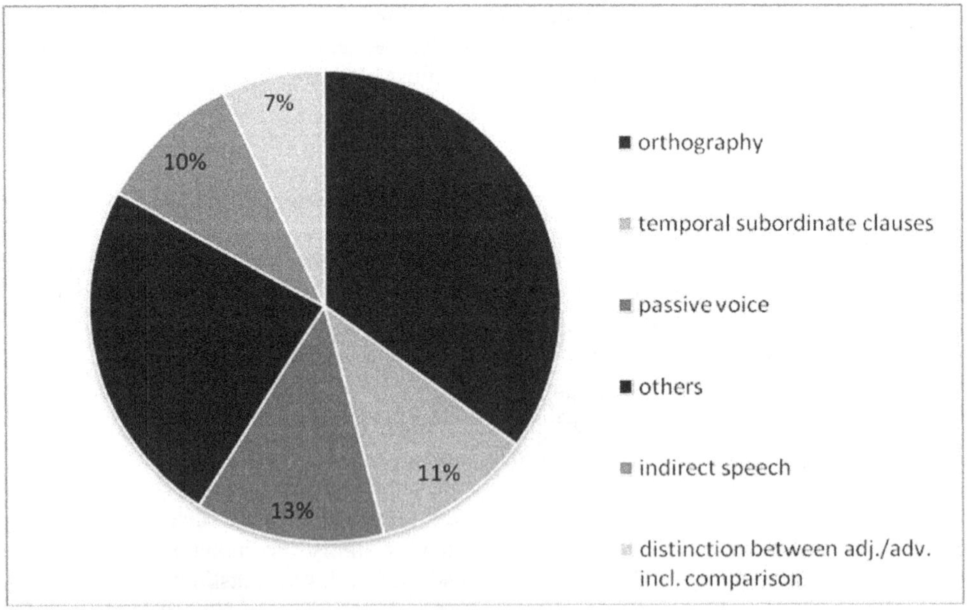

Figure 9.3: Distribution of mistakes in teaching unit's final error analysis

9.4 Conclusion

Regarding the outcome of the second test in comparison to the initial test, one notices an inversely proportional correlation of text length in relation to the number of mistakes. In spite of an increased word production, learners were able – as already mentioned before – to reduce the amount of mistakes especially in those fields of grammar that had been addressed during this teaching unit. Most notably, concerning the usage of tenses in complex sentences, only about half of the number of mistakes occurred in comparison to the initial test. In this context, it is vital to stress the fact that learners did not deliberately avoid structures that had been problematic before but, quite the contrary, implemented them actively, self-confidently, and appropriately. However, it is not possible to ascribe the learning progress to just one single factor, especially because learning takes place individually and under many different premises. Nonetheless, some indications point to the assumption that the special composition of this teaching unit, especially with regard to an ICMM-based implementation of learning videos, contributed immensely to the broad growth of competences.

Due to consistent learner participation in every planning step, the class gained a high level of activity and transparency, which are referred to as central criteria of effective and sustainable education as has been mentioned above with respect to John Hattie's findings (2009). Owing to manifold and variably accentuated possibilities of (peer-) feedback, learners received – again in line with John Hattie – constant comments of their learning progress as well as continuous recommendations for optimizing their performances. Offering different formats of (online)-tests resulted in an all-embracing exercise scenario that addressed each level of complexity and led to linguistic progress and to an increased level of learners' competence.

During the preparation of topics, the alternation of different learning scenarios and media encouraged learners to constantly use and apply as well as multiply encoded grammar structures. In addition, the creation of videos helped learners to visualize abstract grammatical phenomena. This vivid and motivating way of presentation resulted in a deep neuronal cross-linking with positive effects on learning leading to a marked recall. Furthermore, this effect was intensified by multiple learning-by-teaching components. The fact that the teams independently tried to solve all upcoming respective questions went along with an early establishment of a helping culture within the teams. The challenge of producing videos for the whole class community laid the foundation for positive mutual dependencies which motivated learners to work diligently. The fact that the teacher sought to integrate external learners of different age groups and school systems into the project enabled him to stay primarily in the background and to offer help just as needed. As a result, even in technical challenging working periods, members of the learning group managed to rely on each other as well as to benefit from being coached by older learners.

Consequently, the results seem to indicate that the described modification of the ICMM proved itself to be a constructive method for achieving the learning objective in terms of language competence. In addition, learners were also able to enhance their competences in media, applied geography, as well as social and self-expertise. Moreover, in combination with an independent and appropriate reprocessing and presentation of learning contents, the development of media competence made a valuable contribution with regard to future conduction of technique-based career environments with quick communication channels and specialized working profiles. Finally, the project fostered appreciative communication skills within the teams since learners had to constructively discuss various options in order to agree on one final product. Thus, a key competence for living in a social environment was practiced.

Whether different teaching scenarios could lead to similarly positive or even surpassing results is a debatable point. Currently, a comprehensive study investigating the success of ICMM-based learning scenarios in comparison to traditional ones remains something most desirable – the upcoming doctoral thesis of the author of this article is going to bridge this gap in the future. Nonetheless, it can be assumed that due to less activity and responsibility of learners, a traditional teacher-centered context would have resulted in less motivation which would have impeded learning success. In contrast, competence based scenarios generally have the potential for a target-oriented development of language skills. Yet, one may cast doubt whether a similar level of profound processing and multilayered competence could have achieved without including the above-mentioned learning-by-teaching elements. When interweaving those elements with ICMM-structures, the effective, multi-channel adjusted learning material can serve as a stimulus for a long-lasting learning progress.

Through an analysis of the results of this teaching unit, a variety of similar teaching scenarios comes to mind that might benefit from the previously described modification of the ICMM scenario. Above all, the basic concept is apt for establishing factual knowledge of any kind while simultaneously fostering both personal as well as social competences. Given that the outcome of the preliminary phase is any kind of stimulating teaching material such as videos in combination with short quizzes, learners are offered the chance to subsequently build up a private (digital) library which can be consulted at any time for individual training and repetition, thereby leading to the utmost possible sustainability. In the above-described case, the class might include further grammar topics in their private collection as soon as they are tackled, even during later school years, in order to boost the number of videos at hand. In order to spread the work on many shoulders, it might also be a compelling idea to cooperate with several parallel classes: if each group would head for a certain predefined set of videos, the permanent workload for a single class could be significantly reduced. In addition, if there could be the chance to produce more than just one video per topic, students could try out different versions and therefore various explanations for and approaches to the very same topic.[19]

Among EFL teachers, it is common knowledge that learners of a second language have to cope with several acquisition impediments including (neuro-)psychological obstacles (motivation, learning strategies, organization of mental lexicon, etc.), aspects of semantics and pragmatics (when and how to use the meaning of a word or phrase appropriately), as well as the complex rules of syntax and morphology (rules of word formation, sentence hierarchies, deviations from the basic rules, etc.). The evaluation of the teaching scenario introduced in this article has furnished ample evidence for the conclusion that attempts to visualize grammar in an individualized and creative context promise to be highly effective after all. In this context, it might be seen as a key decision

[19] A variety of further benefits arising from the implementation of the ICM is discussed by Weidmann (2012: 60–66).

to not only expose pupils to static pictures, as recently claimed by Werner Kieweg (2012), but to actively encourage them to produce dynamic sequences on their own. By drawing on this approach, the material helped to anchor the relevant structures in the memory of the students and to foster language competences. Above all, the motivating frame offered by this teaching unit facilitated the students' processing of basic functions inherent in elementary grammar issues. Due to its strong learner orientation within a challenging scenario, the project contributed to the realization and establishment of the hitherto repeatedly claimed change of learning culture:[20] lessons are no longer not only planned according to the essential needs of the students, but are in fact transferred to their own responsibility for the benefit of their self-competence. In addition, the concept also paves the way for a plethora of multidisciplinary cooperation options, not to mention the wealth of chances to broaden the horizons of students. This is especially true for settings where learning videos mirror the results of excursions or expert-interviews, to name only a few examples. Since teachers can rather act as a guide and activator than as a traditional instructor, they can concentrate on individual diagnosis and support during in-class activities. In essence, then, the ICMM variant discussed in the course of this article is capable to suggest answers for a lot of contemporarily discussed problems arising in school contexts and to provide valuable starting points for future developments of approaches towards a more effective and long-lasting learning.

9.5 References

Ambridge, Ben/Lieven, Elena V.M. 2011. Child Language Acquisition. Contrasting Theoretical Approches. Cambridge: Cambridge University Press.

Bartens, Werner. 2012. Krude Theorien, populistisch montiert. In: Süddeutsche Zeitung. 9. September, 44.

Bloom, Benjamin S. 1971. Mastery Learning. In: Block, John H. (ed.). Mastery Learning: Theory and Practice. New York: Holt, Rinehart & Winston. 47–63.

Gerlach, David. 2012. R+e+a+d = Read. Den Leseprozess unterstützen. In: Der Fremdsprachliche Unterricht Englisch 119, 18–23.

Handke, Jürgen. 2013. Beyond a Simple ICM. In: Handke, Jürgen/Kiesler, Natalie/Wiemeyer, Leonie (eds.). The Inverted Classroom Model. The 2nd German ICM-Conference – Proceedings. München: Oldenbourg. 15–21.

Handke, Jürgen/Schäfer, Anna Maria. 2012. E-Learning, E-Teaching und E-Assessment in der Hochschullehre. München: Oldenbourg.

Hasebrink, Uwe/Lampert, Claudia. 2011. Kinder und Jugendliche im Web 2.0 – Befunde, Chancen und Risiken. In: Aus Politik und Zeitgeschichte 3, 3–10.

Hattie, John. 2009. Visible Learning. A synthesis of over 800 meta-analyses relating to achievement. New York: Routledge.

Horstkemper, Marianne. 2006. Fördern heißt diagnostizieren. Pädagogische Diagnostik als wichtige Voraussetzung für individuellen Lernerfolg. In: Diagnostizieren und Fördern (= Friedrich Jahresheft 2006), 4–7.

[20] See Oppenhäuser (2010) and Schmitt (2010).

Kieweg, Werner. 2012. Grammatik visualisieren. Bildimpulse zur Festigung grammatischer Kompetenzen im Englischunterricht. Seelze: Klett-Kallmeyer.

Krumbach-Mollenhauer, Peter/Lehment, Tobias. 2010. Führen mit Psychologie. Menschen effizient und erfolgreich führen. Weinheim: Wiley-VCH.

Leech, Geoffrey et al. 2005. Longman Student Grammar of Spoken and Written English. Harlow: Pearson.

Leupold, Eynar. 2008. A chaque cours suffit sa tâche? Bedeutung und Konzeption von Lernaufgaben. In: Der Fremdsprachliche Unterricht Französisch 96, 2–9.

Loviscach, Jörn. 2013. Videoerstellung für und Erfahrungen mit dem ICM. In: Handke, Jürgen/Kiesler, Natalie/Wiemeyer, Leonie (eds.). The Inverted Classroom Model. The 2nd German ICM-Conference – Proceedings. München: Oldenbourg. 25–37.

Neuman, Delia. 2011. Learning in Information-Rich Environments. I-LEARN and the Construction of Knowledge in the 21st Century. New York: Springer.

Niggli, Alois. 2011. Lernarrangements erfolgreich planen. Didaktische Anregungen zur Gestaltung offener Unterrichtsformen. Aarau: Sauerländer.

Oppenhäuser, Holger. 2010. Erziehung zur Postdemokratie? Kritische Fragen an Demokratiepädagogik und Menschenrechtsbildung. In: Lotz, Mathias/van der Minde, Matthias/Weidmann, Dirk (eds.). Von Platon bis zur Global Governance. Entwürfe für menschliches Zusammenleben. Marburg: Tectum. 209–232.

Schäfer, Anna M. 2012. Das Inverted Classroom Model. In: Handke, Jürgen/Sperl, Alexander (eds.). Das Inverted Classroom Modell. Begleitband zur ersten deutschen ICM-Konferenz. München: Oldenbourg. 3–11.

Schmitt, Sophie. 2010. Die unternehmerische Schule und ihre gesellschaftlichen Implikationen. Hessische Schulpolitik in der Perspektive der Gouvernementalität. In: Lotz, Mathias/van der Minde, Matthias/Weidmann, Dirk (eds.). Von Platon bis zur Global Governance. Entwürfe für menschliches Zusammenleben. Marburg: Tectum. 191–208.

Spitzer, Manfred. 2012. Digitale Demenz. Wie wir uns und unsere Kinder um den Verstand bringen. München: Droemer-Knaur.

Steveker, Wolfgang. 2011 Zeitgemäß unterrichten. In: Sommerfeldt, Kathrin (ed.). Spanisch-Methodik. Handbuch für die Sekundarstufe I und II. Berlin: Cornelsen. 23–48.

Weidmann, Dirk. 2013. Inverting a Competence-Based EFL-Classroom. A Model for an Advanced Learner Activation?. In: Handke, Jürgen/Kiesler, Natalie/Wiemeyer, Leonie (eds.). The Inverted Classroom Model. The 2nd German ICM-Conference – Proceedings. München: Oldenbourg. 155–172.

-----. 2012. Das ICM als Chance für die individuelle Förderung von Schülern?. In: Handke, Jürgen/Sperl, Alexander (eds.). Das Inverted Classroom Modell. Begleitband zur ersten deutschen ICM-Konferenz. München: Oldenbourg. 53–70.

[INT 1] Hessisches Kultusministerium (ed.). 2010. Lehrplan Englisch. Gymnasialer Bildungsgang. Jahrgangsstufen 5G bis 9G und gymnasiale Oberstufe. Hessisches Kultusministerium. http://verwaltung.hessen.de/irj/HKM_Internet?cid=ac9f301df54d1fbfab83dd3a6449af60; last accessed on 06/06/2014.

[INT 2] Council of Europe (ed.). 2001. Common European Framework of Reference: Learning, Teaching, Assessment (2001). Council of Europe. http://www.coe.int/t/DG4/Portfolio/?L=E&M=/documents_intro/Data_bank_descriptors.html; last accessed on 06/06/2014.

[INT 3] Hessisches Kultusministerium (ed.). 2009. Oberstufen- und Abiturverordnung. Hessenrecht. Rechts- und Verwaltungsvorschriften. http://www.rv.hessenrecht.hessen.de/jportal/portal/t/28xh/page/bshesprod.psml?pid=Dokumentanzeige&showdoccase=1&js_peid=Trefferliste&fromdoctodoc=yes&doc.id=hevr-OSt_AbiVHErahmen&doc.part=R&doc.price=0.0&doc.hl=1#focus point; last accessed on 06/06/2014.

[INT 4] Medienpädagogischer Forschungsverbund Südwest (Hrsg.). 2013. JIM-Studie 2013. Basisuntersuchung zum Medienumgang 12- bis 19-Jähriger. Medienpädagogischer Forschungsverbund Südwest. http://www.mpfs.de/fileadmin/JIM-pdf13/JIMStudie2013.pdf; last accessed on 06/06/2014.

[INT 5] Reuell, Peter. 2013. Online learning: it's different. Harvard Gazette. http://news.harvard.edu/gazette/story/2013/04/online-learning-its-different/; last accessed on 06/06/2014.

[INT 6] Giering, Birgit Allhoff, Dirk. 2014. Tablets – Pro und Contra. Medienberatung NRW. http://www.medienberatung.schulministerium.nrw.de/Medienberatung/Lern-IT/ Ausstattung/Tablets/Tablets-Pro-und-Contra/; last accessed on 06/06/2014.

References

Ambridge, Ben/Lieven, Elena V.M. 2011. Child Language Acquisition. Contrasting Theoretical Approches. Cambridge: Cambridge University Press.

Baker, James Wesley. 2000. The classroom flip. Using web course management tools to become the guide on the side. In: Chambers, J.A. (Ed.). Selected Papers from the 11th International Conference on College Teaching and Learning. Jacksonville, Florida. 9-17.

Bartens, Werner. 2012. Krude Theorien, populistisch montiert. In: Süddeutsche Zeitung. 9. September, 44.

Bishop, Jacob Lowell/Verleger, Dr. Matthew A. 2013. The flipped classroom: A survey of the research. In: 120th ASEE annual conference & exposition 6/2013. American Society for Engineering Education.

Bloom, Benjamin S. Mastery Learning. 1971. In: Block, John H. (ed.). Mastery Learning: Theory and Practice. New York: Holt, Rinehart & Winston. 47–63.

Braun, Isabel/Ritter, Stefan/Vasko, Mikko. 2012. Inverted Classroom - die Vorlesung auf den Kopf gestellt. In: DNH - Die Neue Hochschule, Heft 5. 166–169.

Carlisle, Martin C. 2010. Using YouTube to Enhance Student Class Preparation in an Introductory Java Course. Proceedings of SIGCSE '10. New York: ACM. 470–474.

Cormier, Dave/Siemens, George. 2010. Through the open door: Open courses as research, learning, and engagement. Educause, 45(4). 30–39.

Cornelius, Caroline 2001. Gegenseitiges Verständnis in Computerkonferenzen: Voraussetzungen und Folgen konversationaler Kohärenz in Entscheidungsfindungsgruppen im Medienvergleich. Berlin: Waxmann.

Davis, Christine. 2013. Flipped or inverted learning: Strategies for course design. In: Smyth/ Volker (eds.).l Enhancing Instruction with Visual Media: Utilizing Video and Lecture Capture. Hershey, PA: IGI Global. 241-265.

Dewey, John. 1938. Experience and Education. New York: Macmillan Co.

Eirich, Karsten. 2005. E-Learning in der juristischen Ausbildung. In: Juristische Ausbildung (JURA) 2005. 277–284.

Erpenbeck, John/Sauter, Walter. 2007. Kompetenzentwicklung im Netz. New Blended Learning mit Web 2.0. Luchterhand in Wolters Kluwer Deutschland, Cologne.

Fischer, Maike/Spannagel, Christian. 2012. Lernen mit Vorlesungsvideos in der umgedrehten Mathematikvorlesung. In: Desel, Joerg/Haake, Joerg M./Spannagel, Christian (eds.), DeLFI 2012 – Die 10. e-Learning Fachtagung Informatik der Gesellschaft für Informatik e.V.. Bonn: Köllen. 225–236.

Friedrich, Helmut F./Mandl, Heinz. 1997. Analyse und Förderung selbstgesteuerten Lernens. In Weinert, Franz E./Mandl, Heinz (eds.). Psychologie der Erwachsenenbildung, Enzyklopädie der Psychologie. Pädagogische Psychologie Bd 4. Göttingen: Hogrefe. 237–293.

Gerlach, David. 2012. R+e+a+d = Read. Den Leseprozess unterstützen. In: Der Fremdsprachliche Unterricht Englisch 119, 18–23.

Häcker, Thomas. 2004. Mit Portfolios in Projekten expansiv lernen. In: Krause, Dörthe/Eyerer, Peter (eds.). 2004. Projektarbeit mit Ernstcharakter. Ein Handbuch für die Praxis der Aus- und Weiterbildung in Schule und Hochschule. Pfinztal: TheoPrax Stiftung, Fraunhofer Institut für Chemische Technologie. 212–227.

Handke, Jürgen. 2006. The Virtual Linguistics Campus – An Overview. In: Handke, Jürgen/ Franke, Peter (eds.). The Virtual Linguistics Campus – Strategies and Concepts for Successful E-Learning. Münster: Waxmann. 14–36.

Handke, Jürgen/Schäfer, Anna Maria 2012. E-Learning, E-Teaching und E-Assessment in der Hochschullehre. München: Oldenbourg.

Handke, Jürgen/Sperl, Alexander (eds.). 2012. Das Inverted Classroom Model. Begleitband zur ersten deutschen ICM-Konferenz. München: Oldenbourg.

Handke, Jürgen. 2013a. Beyond a Simple ICM. In: Handke, Jürgen/Kiesler, Natalie/Wiemeyer, Leonie (eds.). The Inverted Classroom Model. The 2nd German ICM-Conference – Proceedings. München: Oldenbourg Verlag. 15–20.

Handke, Jürgen. 2013b. The VLC Video Strategy. In: Handke, Jürgen/Kiesler, Natalie/Wiemeyer, Leonie (eds.). The Inverted Classroom Model. The 2nd German ICM-Conference – Proceedings. München: Oldenbourg Verlag. 59–76.

Handke, Jürgen/Franke, Peter. 2013. xMOOCs im Virtual Linguistics Campus: Inhalte, Assessment und Mehrwert. In: Schulmeister, Rolf (ed.). Massive Open Online Courses. Münster: Waxmann. 101–126.

Hasebrink, Uwe/Lampert, Claudia. 2011. Kinder und Jugendliche im Web 2.0 – Befunde, Chancen und Risiken. In: Aus Politik und Zeitgeschichte 3, 3–10.

Hattie, John/Timperley, Helen. 2007. The Power of Feedback. In: Review of Educational Research 77 (1). 81–112.

Hattie, John. 2009. Visible Learning. A synthesis of over 800 meta-analyses relating to achievement. New York: Routledge.

Hilgendorf, Eric. 2005. Juristenausbildung und neue Medien. In: Juristenzeitung (JZ) 2005. 365–373.

Hoppe, Gabriela. 2005. Entwicklungen strategischer Einsatzkonzepte für E-Learning in Hochschulen. Lohmar (u.a.): EulThe.

Horstkemper, Marianne. 2006. Fördern heißt diagnostizieren. Pädagogische Diagnostik als wichtige Voraussetzung für individuellen Lernerfolg. In: Diagnostizieren und Fördern (= Friedrich Jahresheft 2006), 4–7.

Johnson, Larry/Adams Becker, Samantha/Estrada, Victoria/ Freeman, Alex. 2014. NMC Horizon Report: 2014 Higher Education Edition. Austin, Texas: The New Media Consortium.

Jones, Marianne/Shelton, Marilyn. 2006. Developing Your Portfolio: Enhancing Your Learning and Showing Your Stuff. New York & London: Routledge.

Keller, Fred S. 1968. Good-bye, teacher... Journal of Applied Behavior Analysis, 1(1), 79–89. doi:10.1901/jaba.1968.1–79

Kerres, Michael/Schmidt, Andreas. 2012. Zur Anatomie von Bologna-Studiengängen. Eine empirische Analyse von Modulhandbüchern. In: Kerres, Michael/Hanft, Anke/Wilkesmann,Uwe/Wolff-Benedik, Karola (Eds.). Studium 2020. Positionen und Perspektiven zum lebenslangen Lernen an Hochschulen. Munster: Waxmann. 82–97.

Kieweg, Werner. 2012. Grammatik visualisieren. Bildimpulse zur Festigung grammatischer Kompetenzen im Englischunterricht. Seelze: Klett-Kallmeyer.

King, Alison. 1993. From Sage on the Stage to Guide on the Side. College Teaching, Vol. 41, No. 1. Taylor & Francis Ltd.

Krumbach-Mollenhauer, Peter/Lehment, Tobias. 2010. Führen mit Psychologie. Menschen effizient und erfolgreich führen. Weinheim: Wiley-VCH.

Lage, Maureen J./Platt, Glenn J./Treglia, Michael. 2000. Inverting the Classroom: A Gateway to Creating an Inclusive Learning Environment. In: The Journal of Economic Education 31 (1). 30–43.

Largent, David 2013. Flipping a large CSO course: An experience report about exploring the use of video, clickers and active learning. Journal of Computing Sciences in Colleges, 29 (1), 84–91.

Leech, Geoffrey et al. 2005. Longman Student Grammar of Spoken and Written English. Harlow: Pearson.

Leupold, Eynar. 2008. A chaque cours suffit sa tâche? Bedeutung und Konzeption von Lernaufgaben. In: Der Fremdsprachliche Unterricht Französisch 96, 2–9.

Loviscach, Jörn. 2012. Videoerstellung für und Erfahrungen mit dem ICM. In: Handke, Jürgen/ Sperl, Alexander (eds.). Das Inverted Classroom Model. Begleitband zur ersten deutschen ICM-Konferenz. München: Oldenbourg. 25–37.

Loviscach, Jörn. 2013. The Inverted Classroom: Where to Go from Here. In: Handke, Jürgen/ Kiesler, Natalie/Wiemeyer, Leonie (eds.). The Inverted Classroom Model. The 2nd German ICM-Conference – Proceedings. Muenchen: Oldenbourg. 3–14.

Lyman, Frank. 1981. The Responsive Classroom Discussion: The Inclusion of All Students. In: Mainstreaming Digest. University of Maryland, College Park, MD. 109–113.

Miller, Jörg/Meyer, Philip/Ruda, Nadine. 2014. Patterns on Civic Engagement, Service Learning and Campus Community Partnerships from the Program for the Advancement of Service Learning and Social Responsibility of Universities. Proceedings of the 18th European Conference on Pattern Languages of Programs EuroPLoP'13 at Kloster Irsee in Bavaria, Germany

Moeller, Clemens. 2013. Aktivierung in der Studieneingangsphase. Presentation at the Inverted Classroom Conference 2013, Philipps Universität Marburg, Germany. 27/02/2013 http://invertedclassroom.wordpress.com/konferenz2013; accessed on 15/08/2013.

Neuman, Delia. 2011. Learning in Information-Rich Environments. I-LEARN and the Construction of Knowledge in the 21st Century. New York: Springer.

Niggli, Alois. 2011. Lernarrangements erfolgreich planen. Didaktische Anregungen zur Gestaltung offener Unterrichtsformen. Aarau: Sauerländer.

Oppenhäuser, Holger. 2010, Erziehung zur Postdemokratie? Kritische Fragen an Demokratiepädagogik und Menschenrechtsbildung. In: Lotz, Mathias/van der Minde, Matthias/Weidmann, Dirk (eds.). Von Platon bis zur Global Governance. Entwürfe für menschliches Zusammenleben. Marburg: Tectum. 209–232.

Ranieri, Filippo. 2001. Der Computer, mein Repetitor – Die Neuen Medien und die neuen Verwirrungen in der deutschen Juristenausbildung. In: Juristenzeitung (JZ) 2001. 856–861.

Schäfer, Anna Maria 2012. Das Inverted Classroom Model. In: Handke, Jürgen/Sperl, Alexander (eds.). Das Inverted Classroom Model. Begleitband zur ersten deutschen ICM-Konferenz. München: Oldenbourg. 3–11.

Schmitt, Sophie. 2010. Die unternehmerische Schule und ihre gesellschaftlichen Implikationen. Hessische Schulpolitik in der Perspektive der Gouvernementalität. In: Lotz, Mathias/van der Minde, Matthias/Weidmann, Dirk (eds.). Von Platon bis zur Global Governance. Entwürfe für menschliches Zusammenleben. Marburg: Tectum. 191–208.

Schön, Donald A. 1987. Educating The Reflective Practitioner. Toward a New Design for Teaching and Learning. San Francisco: Jossey-Bass.

Schulmeister, Rolf/Metzger, Christiane. 2011. Die Workload im Bachelor: Zeitbudget und Studierverhalten. Eine empirische Studie. Münster: Waxmann.

Schweizer, Karin. 2006. Moderation und Steuerung der netzbasierten Wissens-kommunikation. Frankfurt a. M.: Peter Lang.

Slepcevic-Zach, Peter/Tafner, Georg. 2012. Input - Output - Outcome: Alle reden von Kompetenzorientierung, aber meinen alle dasselbe? Versuch einer Kategorisierung. In: Paechter, Manuela/Schmölzer-Eibinger, Sabine/Stock, Michaela/Slepcevic-Zach, Peter/Weirer, Wolfgang (Eds.). Handbuch Kompetenzorientierter Unterricht. Weinheim/Basel: Beltz. 27–41.

Sliwka, Anne/Frank, Susanne. 2004. Service Learning. Verantwortung lernen in Schule und Gemeinde. Weinheim/Basel: Beltz.

Spannagel, Christian. 2011. Das aktive Plenum in Mathematikvorlesungen. In: Berger, Lutz/-Spannagel, Christian/Grzega, Joachim (eds.). Lernen durch Lehren im Fokus. Berichte von LdL-Einsteigern und LdL-Experten; ein Workshop-Band zum LdL-Tag 2009 an der Pädagogischen Hochschule Ludwigsburg. Berlin: epubli GmbH. 97–104.

Spannagel, Christian. 2012. Selbstverantwortliches Lernen in der umgedrehten Mathematikvorlesung. In: Handke, Jürgen/Sperl, Alexander (eds.). Das Inverted Classroom Model. Begleitband zur ersten deutschen ICM-Konferenz. München: Oldenbourg. 73–81.

Spannagel, Christian/Spannagel, Jana. 2013. Designing In-Class Activities in the Inverted Classroom Model. In: Handke, Jürgen/Kiesler, Natalie/Wiemeyer, Leonie (eds.). The Inverted Classroom Model. The 2nd German ICM-Conference – Proceedings. München: Oldenbourg. 113–121.

Spitzer, Manfred. 2012. Digitale Demenz. Wie wir uns und unsere Kinder um den Verstand bringen. München: Droemer-Knaur.

Sporer, Thomas/Eichert, Astrid/Brombach, Julia/Apffelstaedt, Miriam/Gnädig, Ralf/Starnecker, Alexander. 2011. Service Learning an Hochschulen: das Augsburger Modell. In: Köhler, Thomas/Neumann, Jörg (Eds.). Wissensgemeinschaften: Digitale Medien – Öffnung und Offenheit in Forschung und Lehre. Münster: Waxmann. 70–80.

Sporer, Thomas/Sippel, Silvia/Meyer, Philip. 2010. E-Portfolios als Assessment-Instrument im Augsburger „Begleitstudium Problemlösekompetenz“. Zeitschrift für Medienpädagogik 18, 1–18.

Steveker, Wolfgang. 2011 Zeitgemäß unterrichten. In: Sommerfeldt, Kathrin (ed.). Spanisch-Methodik. Handbuch für die Sekundarstufe I und II. Berlin: Cornelsen. 23–48.

Weidmann, Dirk. 2013. Inverting a Competence-Based EFL-Classroom. A Model for an Advanced Learner Activation?. In: Handke, Jürgen/Kiesler, Natalie/Wiemeyer, Leonie (eds.). The Inverted Classroom Model. The 2nd German ICM-Conference – Proceedings. München: Oldenbourg. 155–172.

Weidmann, Dirk.. 2012. Das ICM als Chance für die individuelle Förderung von Schülern?. In: Handke, Jürgen/Sperl, Alexander (eds.). Das Inverted Classroom Modell. Begleitband zur ersten deutschen ICM-Konferenz. München: Oldenbourg. 53–70.

Zlotkowski, Edward. 2008. Foreword. In: Dailey-Hebert, Amber/Donnelli-Sallee, Emily/ DiPadova-Stocks, Laurie N. (Eds.). Service-eLearning: Educating for Citizenship. Charlotte, NC: Information Age. 119–129.

Index

www.ingramcontent.com/pod-product-compliance
Lightning Source LLC
Chambersburg PA
CBHW061355240926
51846CB00007B/1420
* 9 7 8 3 1 1 0 3 4 4 1 7 2 *